PUSHING THE "PULL" DOOR

g. dayhoff addley

OR STOP THE CARNIVAL

ISBN: 0-7596-2606-5

This book is printed on acid free paper.

www.1stbooks.com

1stBooks - rev. 04/29/02

ACKNOWLEDGEMENTS

Writing this book has been the culmination of the experiences I was privileged to savor in the various schools in which I taught. All the names have been changed and some descriptions to protect the guilty.

Thanks to all the students, teachers and administrators who put up with me as I was trying to help them along the way. I owe a great deal to Dr. John E. Rogers, Sr., New England's "Father of Black History", who taught me much that I could use in teaching art and life combined with Black History, in general. I thank him posthumously. His many contributions to society shall live forever.

By writing this satire I hoped to bring about the betterment of the educational system so that the same mistakes will not continually be repeated. The problems satirized in this book are universal.

Also greatly appreciated are the many people who proof-read and corrected my chapters as they emerged and for sharing some anecdotes used in this book. Thanks again.

And lastly, my very supportive family for their seemingly endless job of Xeroxing: my long-suffering husband, Jack; our mid-daughter, Robin and her husband, John; our youngest daughter, Darla and her husband, Ken, and our eldest daughter, Dawn, and her husband, Chuck. Thank you for all being there for me.

Gloria Dayhoff Addley
M Art. Ed

TABLE OF CONTENTS

ACKNOWLEDGEMENTS iii

1 RETIREMENT TO PARADISE 1

2 PUSHING THE "PULL" DOOR 7

3 HURRICANE HUGO 26

4 THE ELITE 38

5 THE STAFF OF LIFE 56

6 KNOWLEDGE IS POWER 90

7 CHALK ONE UP 130

8 FOR ART'S SAKE 149

9 MARCHING ON 181

10 THE JOB BANK 191

11 TROUBLE AT CENTRAL 203

12 THE EVENING YEARS 216

ADDENDUM 225

ILLUSTRATIONS

Figure 1 The "Jewel Box" House 3
Figure 2 Pushing the "Pull Door" 6
Figure 3 "Sprucing up the Driver Ed Car" 11
Figure 4 Outdoor Classes 13
Figure 5 "Burning the Building" 15
Figure 6 "My Beamish Boy" 18
Figure 7 "Table Legs Flying" 23
Figure 8 Hurricane Hugo 25
Figure 9 Aftermath 35
Figure 10 "Signs Of The Times" 45
Figure 11 "Changing Of The Guard" 47
Figure 12 "The Mailbox Episode" 59
Figure 13 "The Fights" 61
Figure 14 "The Security Guard" 65
Figure 15 Cleaning Out The Door Locks 67
Figure 16 "The Rocks" 68
Figure 17 "Dozing Domestics" 70
Figure 18 "The Fireburn" 72
Figure 19 In The Trashbin 74
Figure 20 The Letter 75
Figure 21 Drug Free Mural 77
Figure 22 Rat Bite 86
Figure 23 "The Airconditioner Protrusion" 88
Figure 24 "The Ceiling Sails" 95
Figure 25 Drug Free Sports Pin 97
Figure 26 Big Sale Flyer 98
Figure 27 Creative Crafts Sale 99
Figure 28 Pointelism Or Stipple 105
Figure 29 Folding Fan Project 106
Figure 30 The Art Office Popcorn Sale 109
Figure 31 New Books In The Dump 114
Figure 32 He always finishes first 118
Figure 33 "Photos this way" 122
Figure 34 School Scandals 124
Figure 35 The Orange Paper Incident 128
Figure 36 The Arts Class 131
Figure 37 "The Dummy" 138
Figure 38 The Kick 145

Figure 39 Line Designs 152
Figure 40 Scientific Theory 154
Figure 41 Botanical Signs 155
Figure 42 "My Dream House" 160
Figure 43 The Blue Barrels 162
Figure 44 The Black History Mural 165
Figure 45 Handicapped Coloring Book 167
Figure 46 The Library Windows 169
Figure 47 Giant Caribbean Flowers For The Cafeteria 172
Figure 48 Scratchboard 175
Figure 49 Black Artists Worksheet 177
Figure 50 Map on the Door 179
Figure 51 School Map 180
Figure 52 Diamond Jubilee Parade 183
Figure 53 Puerto Rico Friendship Day 185
Figure 54 Black History Conference 188
Figure 55 The Job Bank 190
Figure 56 Central's Race 204
Figure 57 The Letters 210
Figure 58 Accreditation Reporting 212
Figure 59 The Retirement Conference 217
Figure 60 The Central School Experience 219

1

RETIREMENT TO PARADISE

Lori and Bill Artley had spent every vacation since their 1949 wedding searching for a retirement home, doing research from Canada to Florida, and as far west as the Pacific Ocean. Hawaii was too far and Alaska didn't fit the requirements. It had to be warm, with water sports that would lure lots of family and friends to visit, as well as belong to the U.S.A.

Just before the retirement deadline, they had narrowed it down to the Caribbean Islands. They had visited St. John and found it too quiet; St. Thomas was too noisy and St Croix was too reactionary but St. Ursula was just right. Named by Columbus for the patron saint who gathered the 10,000 vestal virgins together for their aborted march to Jerusalem, they found it had everything…their perfect paradise.

Of the wide variety of islands in the Caribbean, each island seemed to have prejudices against non-citizens. They wanted tourists to come, but not to stay permanently. Some islands would not let non-citizens hold any jobs. They preferred to have the tourists decrease the unemployment among their own citizens rather than have them seek gainful employment regardless of superior training. They wanted the influx to HIRE their citizens instead of settling down, supplying themselves more workers. Lori and Bill intended to become part of the community by not only living there but also working. Since this was an American island, they were already citizens and hoped to find jobs that were not as taxing as the ones they had held in the states.

Lori had been an interior designer and didn't want to continue with all the details, quirky clients and dead beat employers. She was glad to find a teaching position available, in which she was certified and could use her Master's degree. She was certified in Driver Education and Art, both courses in which students are self-motivated. The Personnel Director told her it was easier to get an art teacher there than a driving instructor, and asked if she had any preference. Lori liked both, so they set her up at the high school, but neglected to tell her that she couldn't take students out driving until she received her local driving license. She had been driving for 37 years with licenses in four different states but never before on the left side of the road. The Motor Vehicle Manual said newcomers had six months to obtain an island driver's license, but switching to the left lane took a little time to get used to, so she didn't hurry to apply for a new license. After two months another inquiry finally got a round about answer: she should go for her local license. After passing the test with 100%, she was at last given the keys to the Driver Ed. cars. The students were ecstatic as they had been chomping at the bit to drive!

Bill tried several jobs, and finally found everything copacetic as Director of Development for a private prep school. This fitted in with his Master's degree training in Administration, even though it was a lot easier than his past twenty-five years as Dean of Students of the local college in Hartford, Connecticut. The head master told him that this prep school was the "best kept secret" on St. Ursula and it was Bill's job to put it on the map.

Bill was tall, dark haired and reminiscent of the ancient Romans who occupied England for 400 years. His ancestors had come over to America in the mid-1800's and become coal miners. Now he was the first college graduate in his family and had been the Dean of Students at the University of Hartford for the past twenty-five years.

Lori had dabbled in art since she was four years old. Her mother gave her the backs of advertising flyers which came to the house so she could scribble to her heart's content. Later she received her BFA, Master of Art Education, teacher certification and had since dabbled in interior design, sculpture, window display, paintings in all media and crafts of every type, finally succumbing to teaching art in the public schools when her children got to that age. When their three girls reached the age of sixteen she became certified in Driver Education, also, so that they would become better than average women drivers. This was a life or death teaching situation. After all the things they had experienced together, she wanted them to survive.

In becoming part of the community, the Artley's decided to stay out of the local politics, other than voting in the elections. Blacks ran the government and might resent their intrusion. They did join the Public Library, received Senior Citizen cards, and obeyed the laws whenever they could find out what they were. They enjoyed the myriads of rainbow colored flowers that seemed to be always in bloom, the wide skies with "kites" flying all over the island seeking tasty morsels to take home to their nestlings and the expanses of unspoiled sand and surf that seemed to be dispersed at intervals. Whenever there was a rainy sky, one only had to look up for the sunny sky at the far end of the island and head in that direction for the beaches. A local realtor drove them to all the available houses in their price range. One was on top of a hill with wonderful vistas, but the road up there would be impassible to truck up their belongings. Another house had possibilities but was in such run down condition that the relatives who wanted to sell it should have been charging half the price. It showed they hadn't been there for a long time. Some houses were impossible due to the hot bedrooms which were facing west. The Artleys felt the heat by viewing them late in the afternoon when the sun was going down. It would be stifling to try to sleep in that atmosphere.

Figure 1

THE "JEWEL BOX" HOUSE

They learned that the higher the house was on the hill, the more breeze and if you got a place on the water, you had "no-see-ums" come at 6:00 A.M. and P.M. as well as the possibility of sea-robbers coming up in rowboats on the shore when you were away. Other houses had no view of the ocean, and they reasoned that there would be no sense to live on an island if the house couldn't have some view of the water.

Finally they came to a charming jewel box of a house, with a secluded pool. It was high on the side of a hill with a protective cliff to the north, and receiving the breezy tradewinds cutting through the hills from the south. It was a mass of flowers with a mature fruit orchard on the lowest level which in its unkempt status was as thick as a jungle. They knew that a massive cutting job would have to be done, as well as the righting of several steps which erosion had forced down into a gigantic slide. They were told that there was a leak in the plumbing but didn't know where. However they would come down in price so that it was within the Artley's range. It seems it was owned by bank loans and now the couple had divorced. They had sold it six months previously but the perspective buyer's loan did not come through, so the owners were happy that the Artley's had sold their Connecticut home and had all the money in the bank ready and waiting.

It was a seven room masonry house which had been built by a ship builder. You could see his mark when you looked up and saw the ceiling was like the hold of a ship, with a wide gallery (porch) outside the livingroom overlooking both oceans as well as the valley below and a sugar mill there. The broad teak ceiling beams and the teak parquet floors showed a sharp contrast with the white masonry walls. There were five sliding glass doors from one side of the livingroom to the other assuring lots of light as the outdoors came in. At night, the "Emerald City of Oz" lit up down below them, when a huge oil refinery which worked around the clock, became a blaze of diamonds, rubies, topazes and emeralds. Every flower in the botanical gardens seemed to be in bloom on their acre of land and there was a huge flamboyant tree full of its red blooms at one side of the house. On the other was a twenty-five year old mahogany tree. It had been planted at the time of the building.

The Artleys moved in the following October.

The house became wall-to-wall boxes, which arrived while the four parties were signing the Bill of Sale at the bank. It must have been the grapevine that told the movers how to find them in the midst of the signing as they were informed that the container cost $100. each day it cannot be unloaded. The Artleys had to move in the next day, in spite of the fact that the house was only "broom swept."

Bill Artley found that due to the warm climate, he hopped in the pool every fifteen minutes to cool off. He even brought the book he was reading in there, sitting on the bench at one end. Even though he had turned the house down at first because of the pool maintenance, he found the error of his ways when he came to acknowledge the importance of having it. To get him to agree to buying the house, Lori had committed herself to cleaning the pool, but Bill changed his mind and told her, "Now that I know how important it is to have a pool, I feel that I should take care of it's maintenance."

Years later they had the pool tiled so that Bill could keep track of the ph balance of the water, and Lori grouted the tile when the grout finally disappeared, as it seemed to do every five years. They never could find grout which would permanently stay in place.

Bill had sold or given away all his books, and yet as soon as Lori had unpacked the boxes of the books, he read everyone of them. His hobby was reading, and he regularly visited all the libraries of the island.

Bill acted as a "gopher" for the workmen who made over the garage into a studio for Lori' s art work, built shelves and made the house into a home for the Artleys. By going for all the added supplies they needed, Bill saved the carpenter's time and got to know where the roads on the island went. After everything was fixed, he grew lonely up on the hill, reading and talking to the guard dogs all day, while Lori went down to teach school. When a friend called one day with news of a job opening, he went down for an interview.

"I'm in the position of offering you the job of Director of Development, Bill", said the head master.

"Well, I'm in the position of accepting", confirmed Bill.

Both Lori and Bill did their best to meet the challenges which came along. Ninety-nine percent of the prep school graduates went on to colleges, while Central progressed, too. In the ten years Lori was there, the male graduates finally equaled the same number as the females. Some of them received scholarships to go on to college, but many of them dropped out at sixteen to earn money. Brochures and full page newspaper ads brought the prep school to the island's attention finally, while Central had its numbers cut in half when they built a second high school on the island and the over-crowding ceased. Many people, along with Bill and Lori, tried to make a difference.

Figure 2

Pushing the "Pull" Door

2

PUSHING THE "PULL" DOOR

CRACKLE! CRASH! BANG! SMASH! Down came the double plate-glass doors, crushing the skulls of three students and maiming a respected member of the faculty. The steel hinges had finally succumbed to metal fatigue due to the constant badgering of all who entered or exited the Central School library. There was no indication on either door as to whether it should be pushed, pulled, or was locked. Anyone glancing at the pushing and tugging every period of the school day could foresee that this would have to occur someday. Someday they had to break.

Fortunately Mrs. Artley's guardian angel had ushered her into the only store on that Caribbean island which had one set for sale of "PUSH/PULL" signs, made to adhere to glass doors. She took that as an omen, purchasing them. The following morning before classes, Mrs. Artley made her way to the school library and between groups of students entering and exiting, quickly pulled off the protective paper on the "PUSH" sign, and plopped it on the door straight with the metal edging. Then as some other students passed into the library, she was pushed inside and when no one was coming through, ripped off the other protective paper and secured the "PULL" sign in back of the other. One side of the glass now said "PUSH" and the other side "PULL", just at the moment the passing bell sounded and the whole library of students exited for morning classes. Timing is everything!

This scenario was observed by one of the librarians, Mr. Svenske, who made his way over to the door and told Mrs. Artley that those signs would be down in a week. Central School students usually removed everything that was not painted on the wall. Each day Mrs. Artley checked if the signs were still there. They were. The students must have realized that by leaving them there, they were saving their own lives. The inevitable door crash had been averted just in time.

Years later one of the signs was removed, but since the back of the other one showed black through the glass, Mrs. Artley took her "white out" and lettered "PUSH" on the other side of it. She wasn't an art teacher for

nothing! No one even knew the difference and the signs remained there as long as the glass doors.
Due to the destruction of hurricane Hugo, much of the library needed to be replaced, including the glass doors. Mrs. Artley was happy to see that the "PUSH/ PULL" was engraved in the new glass doors. The school had come a long way.

Another part of the library which needed replacing after Hugo was the roof. Hugo had removed over 90% of the island's roofs and when the roof leaks in a library, the books are ruined. Mr. Svenske was ever vigilant and came to the school's rescue immediately. Neglecting his own personal repairs at home, he moved shelves of books at school to the few dry areas, and then, along with the other librarians, packed up the good books placing them in a dry area. Many books were already damaged, but due to his quick response the school saved a nucleus of books for their "new" library. Later, the Federal Government sent Central 6,000 new books and two computers with which to catalog them. (And a few brainless politicians vociferously sounded off about severing relations to become a "free" country! What would the island do in a disaster like Hugo with no Federal Government? If only this little Caribbean island had an insane asylum, these crazies could be locked up, and the key could be thrown in the ocean.)

About a month after the hurricane, school reopened even though it was still unsafe for everyone. There was no running water, the cement blocks on the walls were cracked ready to fall on the unsuspecting and electrical wires hung down all over the place. It was a good thing the electricity was out for over six months. The soggy acoustical carpeting in the library needed to be removed, and the metal turnstiles at the check-out counter were rusted. Unfortunately when Mr. Snow, the school maintenance man, removed them, he left three bolts sticking up out of the floor, which he said, "couldn't be removed". Everyone fell over them, but instead of finding a way to pull them out, he covered them with a see-saw board. This was worse than the bolts!

One day when Mrs. Artley was leaving the library after doing some research on Black History for her classes, the see-saw had been put aside. Since there was nothing to call attention to the three bolts Mrs. Artley fell over them spraining her shoulder badly and hitting her head on the glass doors. She had to be taken to the hospital and was out of school for some time. After she came back, it was therapy each day after school til the end of the term. She couldn't move her left arm.

Within half-an-hour of her fall, Mr. Snow removed those three "unremovable" bolts.

Seven years later Workman's Compensation called Mrs. Artley to verify the charges. It seemed they still had not paid the doctor.

They were pushing the "PULL" door, as usual.

IT'S HARD TO GET A DRIVER ED TEACHER HERE

SEXUAL HARASSMENT! The man who filled the Driver Ed car with gas was jealous of Mrs. Artley's job. He had to stay there and pump gas all day instead of driving around with the pretty young high school students. He did everything to delay them when they drove in for gas. Somedays he pumped it in drop by drop until the other government cars in the line up finally complained. He put his whole body through the window and into the car to talk to the girls. When Lori turned to sign for the gas, he picked up a broomstick and pointed it from his groin at her back, as if to rape her. His buddies looked on, hooting and smirking. Once, she had to restrain Alphonso, a male student, from fist fighting with him. Mrs. Artley had to write several letters to his superiors. Each time he retaliated making her teaching unbearable and forcing her to tears.

Finally she learned of a place about 20 miles away where government cars could also get gas. This made it impossible to take students with her as they would not get back to school in time for the next period, but at least the man was normal, so she went after school. The only trouble was if she went on pay day he took time off to cash his paycheck. Then he was gone all afternoon.

Lori had two classroom groups of twenty students each, and there was one other Driver Ed teacher, Mr. Bastet, who did the same. Only eighty Driver Ed students per term plus doing nine class periods on the road with each student made it a very expensive course, but it was cheaper than putting new drivers out on the roads untrained.

With Alphonso at the wheel, driving routine was mapped out containing nine different driving situations. Starting out in a nearby empty parking lot to which Lori would drive the beginners, they drove in circles to see the curve of their wheel base, both forward and backward. Then they had to practice steering by driving around the perimeter both forward and backward. The students learned starting, stopping, steering and SAFETY.

The second lesson involved learning how to park in a slot in that parking lot. The students usually could drive from the school about a block away and back by then, mingling with the traffic flow. When they became good at parking without cars around, they moved to an adjacent lot where there were other vehicles. The students never touched another car as they could see the gravity of the situation, and they became very good parkers. The only trouble was that their car was well marked "DRIVER EDUCATION". When people saw the marked car, they suddenly decided to move theirs. Perhaps they recalled how terribly they parked when they were learning. New drivers often parked in unmarked cars with family or friends in those same parking lots and the worried people never moved their vehicles, not even realizing the risk. Their home cars never even had a dual-control brake installed as the professional cars did.

Mrs Artley continued with a format of one lesson in slant-in and parallel parking, left side and right, alternating with one lesson in country or city driving. She also did a mock shopping trip, so the students learned about planning a trip before one starts to avoid crossing streets unnecessarily plus all types of safe parking. The end lesson was back in the same parking lot in which they started, doing hazard avoidance this time. The students loved that lesson as cones were placed across their path, and just before passing through them, Mrs. Artley would tell them to switch to lane A, B, or C to "avoid a collision", at the last minute. There were other hazards and then parallel parking between the cones to finally see if they were ready to take their driving tests. Quick decisions!

The driving inspector hated to spend much time with such well prepared students. They always came through with flying colors but Lori insisted that the inspectors should be "tough" with them. Arranging for someone to come up to the school to give the written test was usually more difficult, but it saved about eighty students from missing school for a morning and most had no means of transportation. The Motor Vehicle

Department was about a mile from the bus stop and they only gave the test at 9:00 A.M. on Thursdays.

The students also had to have an eye and medical test and fifteen dollars. Lori had Xeroxed the forms so they could have it all filled out by one doctor, eliminating the cost of going to an eye doctor separately. This was costly enough for them.

Figure 3

"Sprucing up the Driver Ed Car"

One time a tall black student named Jason who was mistrusting of all white people, had forgotten to get his fifteen dollars from his parents before leaving home that morning. No one he knew would have that kind of money to loan him. When Lori learned of the situation, checked her wallet and saw there were fifteen dollars, she presented them to him in low key. His eyes opened wide, and he accepted it reluctantly but appreciatively. He passed his test, and the next day returned the money, as well as came into her room after school and asked if she had any stapling or other jobs he could do. She really didn't but found something he could do. She could see that he thought he was "beholden" to her. Jason was a very proud young man.

There were times when the school vehicles were unusable due to the need for replacement parts or flat tires. Lori found that it took months for the repair department to requisition parts as the invoices required seven signatures. When the parts finally were put in months later, she could start driving again. When it came to flat tires, she and Mr. Bastet footed the bill themselves. They were fixed in fifteen minutes.

What a waste of everyone's time! In order to pay for these minor repairs, which added up over time, they decided to charge ten dollars to students who chose to use the school cars for their driving test at the Motor Vehicle Department. This did take their time driving to and from the Motor Vehicle Department, as well as waiting while the test was in progress.

Even the vice-principal of the school wanted his son to take his driving test on the school vehicle. It seemed to Lori that a parent who really cared about a son or daughter would want to be part of this "right of passage" if at all possible.

All those who participated in the course could see that Driver Education was a real life-saving and a very relevant course, to which prospective drivers of every age should be exposed. This was not only for the learner's benefit but for all those already driving on the highways. Not only should teenagers experience driver education but all NEW drivers of all ages. Lori knew from experience that the older a person was, the MORE s/he needed Driver Education. The younger students were more open to doing everything they were told and remembering it, while older students forgot important things like parking and Y-turns. They also fought learning, had slower reactions and didn't use new innovations such as seatbelts and shoulder harnesses. Those who learned from untrained family members may find that they have learned to turn left first when making a right hand turn (or vice verse) or they experience someone taking them out on a freeway for their FIRST lesson.

Scarred for life, they continue to have crashes throughout their driving career and don't understand why.

Since driver education was such a meaningful course, the Department of Education decided to DROP it! The reason given to Mrs. Artley was that the very high insurance premiums were due and since the cars were now five years old, the insurance company would not renew.

Lori felt they could have switched the five-year-old cars with a couple of two-year old government cars. Also, if they really wanted to cut costs, they should have hired only one teacher to teach the classroom phase for five periods a day (about 125 students). Then they could have used two para-professionals to do the road work. This would more than double the number of students for the teacher and the drivers could be driving all day during the student's free periods. As an added bonus, it would assure that trained drivers would be out on the roads driving for SAFETY.

Figure 4

Outdoor Classes

There is no other time in a person's life where a "captive audience" is raring to learn about SAFETY on the highways—lifesaving skills. By canceling, Lori Artley knew they were really pushing the "PULL" door again.

BUMPED OUT INTO TEACHING ENGLISH

FIRE! FIRE! The Fine Arts Building was on fire! Three students were seen by a custodian. They were running from the fire they started in the waste basket of a second story room. The culprits were caught but the building burned to the ground. As far as anyone knew, the students only got a smack on the wrist for punishment. It was three days before the embers stopped smoldering.

This left the already overcrowded school short twelve classrooms housed in that building. The administration didn't know what to do.

The Driver Education room was over in the gym, with an adjoining office inside the room. A few days later a math teacher from the burned building, who Mrs. Artley had never seen before, came at the beginning of one of her classes, informing her that this room was now "his". Mrs. Artley told him that she had no notification of this and until she did, this room was still "hers". He left.

The next day Mrs. Artley received notification that her classes had been "bumped out" to nowhere.

There was no way to teach a class in the bleachers of the gym...too many distractions and too noisy. Canvassing the campus, Lori found a shady spot under a spreading flamboyant tree. Two benches nearby could be moved there to form an "L" and she could bring in some beach blankets from home to make enough room for a class. Pulling her car up to that spot, she opened the hatchback to reveal a large pad of newsprint for her chalkboard. The students were reluctant to sit down, at first, until plastic table cloths were laid across the benches. Finally one of the young men swooped down to the beach blanket on the ground and spread out showing its spacious comfort. The rest of the "standees" followed his lead, and the class settled in to continue their Driver Education studies. Several times the students had to run for cover when it rained, but that only lasted about ten minutes, so class was resumed when the down pour was over. It turned out to be the best class yet because they finished the whole text book and the driving manual without any driving lessons to interfere. Everything meshed together and the students received certificates for the classroom phase but had to take their driving portion from a commercial driving school at their own expense.

Figure 5

"Burning the Building"

Toward the end of the first semester when attending a PTA meeting, a distraught mother stood up and told of her dilemma: It seemed that several of the English teachers had left in midyear for various reasons, and her son's English teacher had joined the National Guard and was called to go. English—a required subject for graduation! His mother almost cried. If he missed English that year, he was not allowed to take two years of English simultaneously, so he would have to miss graduation and have it afterward.

Lori was present at that P.T.A. meeting and couldn't help but take pity on her. Mrs. Artley would be "free" the following term since Driver Ed had been dropped. Even though she was not certified to teach English, it was her native language and she <u>was</u> certified in teaching. She firmly believed that if you learned how to teach one subject, the same principles could easily be applied to other subjects.

The next day, Lori went to the principal and offered her services. Soon she was assigned a new room and English classes. Two were regular English classes and one was called Creative Writing. She was also teaching two art classes already, in order to free up Ms Lash, who then became the head of the Art Department. Chairpersons have a lighter teaching load due to their departmental duties.

Then Mrs. Artley discovered that one of the English classes was an Advanced English class and the other Standard. That meant that while one was concentrating on "poetry", for example, the other learned "grammar". The Creative Writing course was not supposed to be creative as much as it was supposed to be remedial. This gave her three different lesson plans to prepare each evening, beside the one she was already doing for the art classes. The norm is TWO. She was VERY busy that Spring and not even certified in English.

One day in the advanced English class, one bright student piped up, "How can you teach English when you weren't trained to do it?" At the beginning they had been told that she was not certified to teach English, but that she was doing it so that they would not "miss" a semester and thereby could graduate on schedule. There was no certified English teacher available at that time.

Mrs. Artley answered his question, "When I was in high school, I listened". The whole class applauded that answer, and Lori chalked up a big one for herself.

After that they all got along fine. Her students, helped her and she helped them.

One requirement which everyone enjoyed was the study of Shakespeare's "Julius Caeser". One kind and generous English teacher, Ms. Queenie, took pity on her ignorance and gave her an excellent outline of the play. Passing it along to her students before they read the play, made it all make sense. All the students took turns reading parts, and one girl enjoyed that so much she expressed the desire to become an actress when she graduated.

In the Creative Writing class, Lori Xeroxed the pages of their workbooks nightly, which were corrected during class the next day by the students. They also created individual magazines, according to their interests and made colorful covers in class using magic markers and collages cut from other magazines. Included were a table of contents, an editorial on their favorite subjects plus whatever else they wished to put in. The illustrations were rudimentary or else cut-outs. Other students in the room read the magazines avidly as Lori hung them above the chalkboard. When the chairperson came to see if they had anything to contribute to the English Fair, held at another school, she was surprised to find such CREATIVE writings and selected ALL of them to proudly display. When they were returned, much to the dismay of one student, one of the magazines had been stolen. Someone wanted a sample.

Lori was just glad that they had produced something unusual enough to be of value. It was a compliment to have even been asked to contribute.

One day in Mrs. Artley's advanced English class, she was introducing poetry. Fortunately she had just finished a "Children's Literature" course at the local college and all the forms of poetry were illustrated in their book. Lori Xeroxed this for them, and recited a few poems she knew by heart to get them started. Right in the middle of the "Jabberwocky" from Alice in Wonderland, when at the climatic part she enunciated with emphasis, "Come to my arms my beamish boy", an unknown young man came into the room with a notice for all teachers. To his bewilderment, she was stretching out her arms to him. By the time he reached the desk and left the notice for her, she finished the poem, "O fraptuous day, Caloo, Callay, he chortled in his joy".

Figure 6

"My Beamish Boy"

The timing was more perfect than if it had been planned, and the class applauded again.

After she had finished that grand introduction (with straight man), Mrs. Artley had no trouble getting the students to choose poems from their English books which they could read aloud expressively, then explain and tell about the author...for a grade.

They also wrote creative poetry, especially the "diamente" style, which didn't have to rhyme but had to have the correct count and balance of meter. Some of these were so good they should have been published. This class was filled with "born successes"

They were really pushing the "<u>PUSH</u>" door, that time.

Sun
Warmth; Fruits; Green grasses
Growing things; Hills; Valleys; Flowering
Rocks; Rivers; Waterfalls; Freezing rains; Volcano
Floods; Tornados; Hurricanes; Typhoons
Mudslides; Earthquakes; Cold
Darkness

Clouds
Palm fronds waving
Smooth river rocks; Burbling brooklets
Rainbow of flowers; Polination; Buzzing bees
Animal waste on dust dry roads
Hurricane winds
Storms

DIAMENTES

New born
Little, Carefree
Active, Learning, Doing
Successful, Joyful, Moving, Youthful
Sedatory, Hunched, Pill popping, Old
Knowledge, Inept, Failing
Arthritic, Pained
Dying

Seed
sun, earth, rain
fertile, growing, flowering, food
fruits, vegetables
more seeds

EARLY SCHOOL YEAR STRESS

A shortage of everything...and it was the first day of school! They had had all summer to order furnishings, books, supplies, fix things, school maintenance and get needed teachers but nothing had been done! The principal accounted for this by saying that some things HAD been done over the summer, but that there were so many things to attend to that those few things didn't show. In reality it was that the school administration would leave at the end of June and vacation until the end of August. Sometimes the government would provide jobs for teenagers over the summer, such as painting, but they left the supervision to the one maintenance man who would evidently show them what to paint, and leave. Such sloppy painting has never been seen! Drips on the walls and floor; breaking door locks; painting OVER glass windows and they never had heard of using masking tape or a mask when one color butts up against another.

Because so much was in disarray it always took over a month at the beginning of the school year to register enrollment and to get the necessary furniture in the rooms before really starting to teach. Lori's heart ached for the good students who came to their classes the first day and expected to learn something. They had to listen to the repetition of the class expectations, introduction of the new students each day and do "busy" work as no project could be started before the whole class could participate. Some teachers didn't even bother to keep their classes busy, so the students would just sit, talk and do nothing. Others, like Mrs. Artley, started the first project but didn't count it as compulsory until the whole class had arrived. Everyone was accountable, however, when the class was tested on what they had learned from that project, the students who had spent more time did better on the tests.

There was a room shortage for about seven years after the Fine Arts Building was burned down, and Lori was shuttled all over the campus, even to not having any room for a while. Finally the first floor of the Fine Arts Building was rebuilt and she was scheduled to have one of the brand new rooms. The only problem was that was all...a room. There was a teacher's desk and chair in it, but it became exceedingly stressful when 27 students began to arrive every period with no seats or desks for them.

It was even worse when they placed an ill mannered English teacher, Ms. Feelbad, there during Lori's free periods. Lori could not even unpack the boxes of art materials her fellow teachers had graciously carried down from her previous room. Ms. Feelbad was too insecure to hold class while Lori was still in the room. She believed in "cussin" students out in their same vulgar vernacular as Ms. Feelbad felt that it was the only language students understood. Mrs. Artley had to unpack her art supplies after school, and put the things away in the same metal cabinets which she had brought from her last room. She finally figured out a way to lock the cabinets with truck chains so that the things wouldn't get stolen.

Meanwhile, Mrs. Artley had to get chairs so that her students could at least sit down when they came in the room. Although the English students used the chairs also, there was never any effort put forth by Ms. Feelbad to bring any chairs into the room or any recognition of Lori's efforts.

After school each day Lori took her hatch back around the campus and put whatever chairs had been left outside rooms into the back. Then she drove them back and carried them in. In the meantime, she would also bring in whatever folding chairs she had at home to be used until enough chairs for the students were retrieved from outside the classrooms. She also raided the broken chair store room which filled up a teacher's lounge so the teachers couldn't even get through. Lori marked all the chairs with her room number on the back, so that no one could come and claim them after all her hard work. Some other rooms must have been left "short" but Mrs. Artley was desperate. Students deserved at least a seat in the classroom!

Then there was the matter of desks. A student couldn't draw very well without tables or desks, unless they had sketch pads (which they didn't). Since the administration failed to take notice of the fact that artwork could not be carried on with no desks, the iniative of obtaining tables was left up to the teacher. At home, Lori had three sheets of plywood. She hired a man with a truck to meet her at lunch time and carry the plywood down to the school where she had her students unload it as they came to class. They were placed on saw horses, and covered with some large picnic table cloths which she had from the past. In order to do all this in the one-hour lunch period, they all had to synchronize their watches and meet at exact times. It all worked out just as the bell rang. They put the chairs around the make-shift tables and the art class finally was in business!

The class was crowded with nine students at each table but they didn't complain. In the following week after school Mrs. Artley painted both sides and edges of each table, as they were of "outside" plywood which has poison injected so the bugs won't eat it. The paint sealed it in. If she didn't do this, the administration would undoubtedly have noticed!

Finally after months passed the principal, Mr. Buffalo-soldier, informed Mrs. Artley that there had been a trailer load of Junior High desks on campus all this time. He said her students could go down and each bring a desk/chair combination, which fit, back to the art room. Why didn't he tell her this the first day of school when she told him the predicament? The next day they went down to get the desks, although the larger students couldn't fit into the Junior High desks. They put the plywood vertically against the wall to make bulletin boards, and then eventually it was cut into much needed shelves for the art office.

The school lunchroom was next door, and Mrs Artley noticed pieces of several tables which they had thrown outside. She went over and selected the parts of two tables and carried them back to the room to be used by the larger students who couldn't squeeze into the Junior High desks. The next day she brought in Bill's electric drill, some three-inch screws and the electric screwdriver from home.

At lunch, several students helped her fix the tables. They loved working with the power tools and the only problem they encountered was that one table had two of its legs put on backward, by someone else. The students couldn't get the legs off to fix them. Even though the legs were facing the wrong way they used the table as there was a desperate need.

Soon after this, Mr. Past, one of the vice-principals, commandeered the two tables. They had to be used for a special program in the cafeteria. This was done several times a year to all the rooms with tables in them. The only problem was they always took them but NEVER returned them! They also didn't tell time length so it was assumed that they would never be returned. The tables were needed in the classrooms in order to teach. Without them, the students sitting at them couldn't do their work.

Due to this, Mrs. Artley went over to the cafeteria at the end of the day. Using her electric screw driver, she unscrewed all the three-inch screws she had brought to secure the legs and without a word, she left. How surprised they would be when they tried to move the tables.

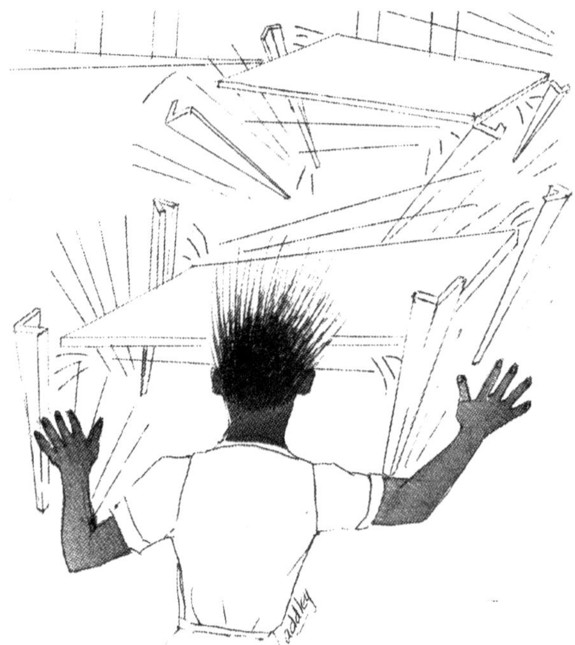

Figure 7

"Table Legs Flying"

Lack of communication was the cause.

Ms. Feelbad and Mrs. Artley only spoke to each other when absolutely necessary, even though they shared the same room. The reason was a deliberate misunderstanding. Another lack of communication.

Lori found out later that Ms. Feelbad prided herself on always being late for her own classes...sometimes even fifteen minutes. Since Mrs. Artley had so many boxes to unpack, she tried to do some of this at the end of a class period, before Ms. Feelbad came in. Since the room was airconditioned, the English class would come inside to wait for Ms. Feelbad, as sometimes it was very warm outside in the tropical climate. After about fifteen minutes, Ms. Feelbad came in, and Lori left so the remainder of the period might be spent with her class.

After class she sought Mrs. Artley out in the hall and said to her face, "You're trying to f _ _ k around with me."

When Mrs. Artley got over the initial shock of her words, she pulled herself together and countered without batting an eye, " First of all, I never try to f _ _ k around with women, and secondly, if I were an English teacher, I wouldn't use vulgar language". She resented having to use this vulgar word which was not in her normal vocabulary, but she felt Ms. Feelbad should "hear" how she sounded and might realize how unfitting that word was.

There was further heated exchange which ended by Ms. Feelbad saying that her students were to wait outside in the tropical climate for her late arrival each day. It ended by them telling each other to "Drop dead", and Ms. Feelbad had to have the last word saying that Mrs. Artley would probably drop dead before she did.

With things like death, one NEVER knows until it happens!

The whole scenario was documented in Lori's typewritten letter to Mr. Buffalo-soldier plus two vice-principals. When Ms. Feelbad was confronted in the principal's office, she denied EVERYTHING in front of Mrs. Artley, who knew the truth. Lori had to call her the liar that she was. She must have realized she was a liar as Ms. Feelbad did not retort...and she always had to have the last word.

At the end of the school year, when they were alone in the teacher's lounge, Ms. Feelbad apologised for the way she had acted. She told Lori that she was not the same person she was at the beginning of the term and now she had found religion and had been "born again".

She will never know how much she added to the school-year stress Lori, as well as the rest of the school, had experienced. Perhaps she had started pushing the "<u>PUSH</u>" door, at last.

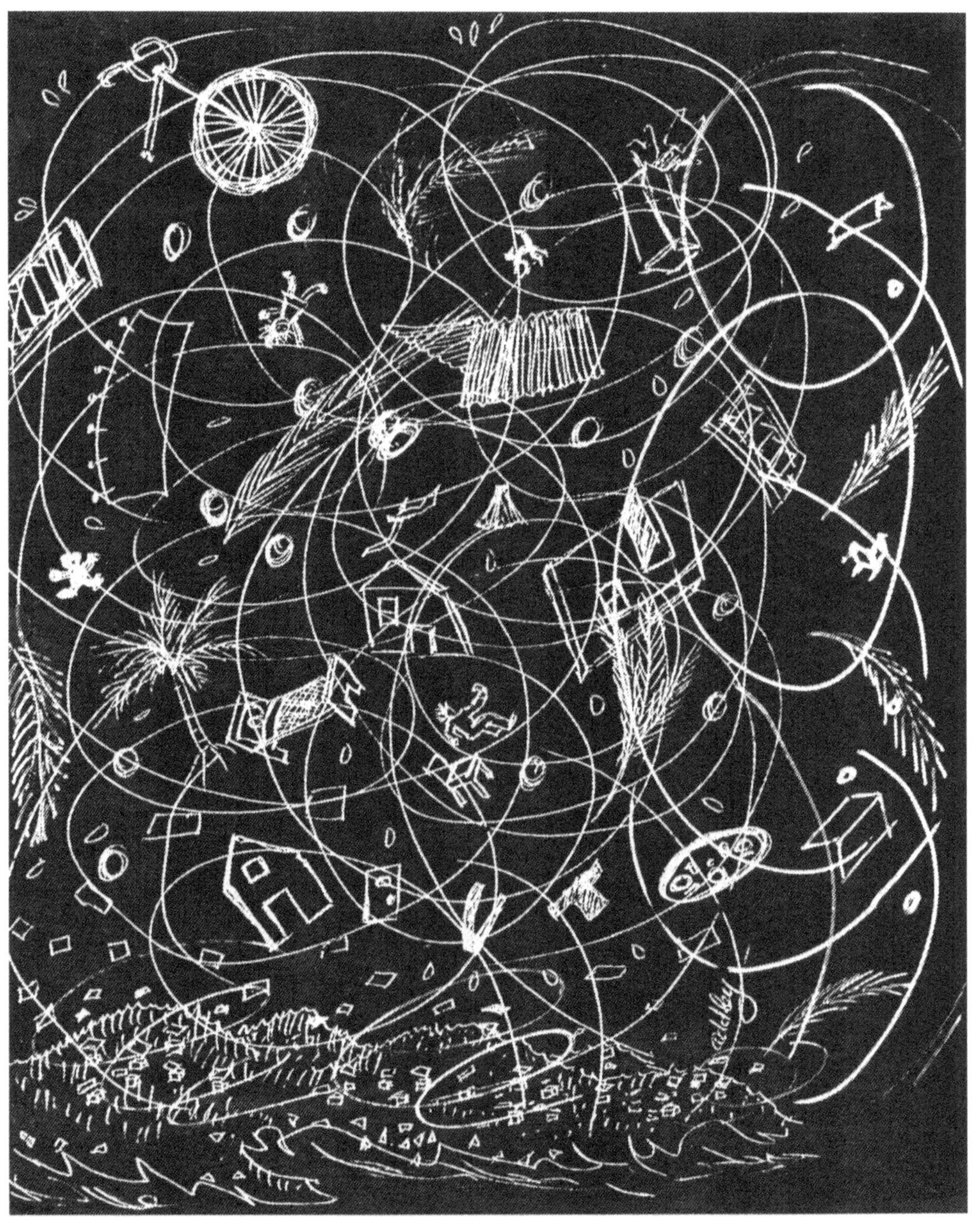

Figure 8

HURRICANE HUGO

3

HURRICANE HUGO

In the fall of 1989, Central High School and the island experienced fifteen hours of Hurricane Hugo, stopping its 240 mph winds, plus tornadoes, right over St. Ursula Island, rampaging roofs, whole houses and everything in its path. It was said to have been the most violent storm of the century. After Hugo finally moved along the next morning, they experienced an aftermath of rain and winds for over a week. If houses hadn't completely blown away, 95% of the roofs went, the glass broke and everything got soaked.

Many of the classrooms at Central lost their roofs. Some of the classrooms and the main office also lost their walls leaving anything that was still left inside vulnerable. Even the school gymnasium, which was a "designated shelter" for people needing a "haven" from the storm, collapsed and those inside had to crawl on their hands and knees in the dark of night with the storm raging around to find some place to wait out the hurricane. Those who crawled to the main office found it was also demolished, but right across the street, a church was still standing and untouched. The minister of that church was a master-builder and had constructed that church, with the help of his congregation, to withstand the winds. The people who weathered out the storm inside were safe. All over the island there were "pockets" where the buildings were unaltered, while in most other places, everything blew away. If Hugo wanted some building, he got it!

Hugo also touched the other islands in its path: Guadelupe, Monserrat, Antigua, St. Martin, Dominique, St. Kitts, Nevis, the Virgin Islands, Puerto Rico and finally on to the states. He left crippling and crushing in his wake; all plants disappeared. The landscape looked like no-man's land.

Those who had not been touched tried to send help to those wounded, as they knew it would be a long time before the island would return to where it had been before. Even Guam sent electricians and construction workers; they knew how it was. St. Ursula Island did come back even stronger than before. Since the people could no longer get insurance, Lori and Bill decided to put that money into hurricane-proofing their home. They did everything they learned they should have done: steel ceiling ties to the roof, three inch screws holding roof down to beams, heaviest steel braces, shoring up weak spots, silicone paint on the roof to form a skin, tempered glass and less glass to break wherever possible, grills on every opening and hurricane shutters bolted down over the grills. Few knew how to do this before as it had been 78 years since the last big hurricane and probably there would never be another one as bad a Hugo.

The day before the big hurricane was delightful – cooling trade winds and sunshine; flowers all over the island. They had been warned that a hurricane was coming, but many people didn't believe it would really happen this time. Even when they did, they didn't really know HOW to prepare. Just a speck on the map, too many times before the island had been alerted with hurricane warnings, only to have the storm veer to the north at the last moment. There was almost a frivolous mood in some houses before it hit. When the sky darkened; the winds started blowing; people closed their hurricane shutters; some played family games until the electricity went off; other prayed and some laid down but there was no sleeping. The loudest noise ever heard came like a locomotive running over them...for fifteen hours straight.

After daylight came the noise lessened but on inspection all hanging things were now on the ground; all walls were covered with small fragments of debris; all glass was broken slashing the drapes and covering the floor; cardtable tops, pot lids and other loose objects had blown out the now open windows; the new bag of dry dogfood was soggy mush on the wet livingroom rug and there were two inches of water all over the parquet floors. In the guest room the bed had been blown across the room to the now broken glass doors and would have been the next thing tossed in the winds if the hurricane had stayed.

Most hurricane shutters blew away within the first five minutes leaving large segments of corrugated steel flying in the wind along with the coconuts and pieces of furniture and houses. The frenzied, smacking, slamming emulsion blew around the island, adding to the damage the tornadoes within did by themselves. Many of the damages were caused by those flying pieces hitting houses, cars and animals left outside. Destruction to the environment was greater than the military men who came to help the recovery, had ever seen even in combat zones. The Red Cross, FEMA and SBA workers said this was the worst they had ever encountered.

When Lori and Bill apprehensively opened their doors in the dim morning light all they could see was barren devastation. Every tree was bare, broken and devoid of branches and leaves. Where did the birds go? Some survived returning later but were still invisible that first day. In the weeks that followed, Lori observed a Rhode Island red hen with a freshly hatched brood of chicks coming out from under floor boards of a former home and teaching them how to scratch for food. Her house and all other signs of civilization had blown away, but there she was, starting life anew. Did she even realize a hurricane had just come by?

The day before, this island had been a lush green tropical paradise. A day later the entire area looked like a "war zone" after a war. Bill thought he was having a heart attack so he had to lie down. What would they feed their dogs after the mush turned rancid? "Should everyone just give up", Lori wondered, "or should they take a tip from the Rhode Island red hen and start anew?"

With inner strength and the help of God, Lori started to pick up the pieces.

It was two weeks before Lori had time to pick up the parts of the door to her antique mahogany china closet and found that the pieces had been ripped off the hinges and unglued. In her exhausted state she put them in a plastic garbage bag.

"This should keep them out of the two inches of water on the wooden floors," thought Lori. Then she realized her feet were cold, soaked to the bone and she went to find the old waterproof mukluks she had worn after skiing. She thanked God that she still had them. Her hands were a series of cuts and bruises from picking up the splinters of glass. She found a pair of thick workman's gloves in order to continue. With the help of a wheelbarrow, each day she dumped the glass into the ravine next to the house. After all, she reasoned, glass is made from sand and should eventually return to its origin.

With gargantuan strength Lori rolled up the soggy rugs and dragged them out to hang on the wrought iron railing. The Artley's middle daughter, Robin with her husband, found their detoured way to their parent's house, and helped clean up the debris in their yard. Robin signed up with FEMA to be the "agent" for that area and received some huge tarpaulins, with which to cover the roofs and keep out the rain. It rained sporatically for two weeks after Hugo.

Feeling slightly better finally, Bill drove half across the island to make an appointment with their insurance adjuster. These inspectors were sent in from the states and had no idea of directions. Bright and early Bill drove down the next day at 7:00 A.M. and led him up into the mountains to their house. Several of the insurance companies on the island went bankrupt, but fortunately Continental Insurance Company came through for them, paying for their huge damages a short time afterward. It covered their losses and at least they had a house in which to live.

There was no electricity for over three months, so Lori had to learn to cook on a camp stove. This was no easy task since she had never gone camping.

One day Lori and Bill looked out into the beautiful panorama of both the Caribbean on the south and the Atlantic Ocean on the north, sparkling in the sunshine and they heard buzz saws and hammering. Lori looked around and there was no evidence of rebuilding on her house. All the workmen were busy rebuilding their own houses. She decided then and there that she must go back to Connecticut and bring down carpenters and supplies. After making arrangements she took off for a week and stayed with their eldest daughter, Dawn and her husband, Chuck in Southbury, Connecticut. Visiting various hardware shops and buying supplies to send home, Lori inquired about getting in touch with two carpenters who would be willing to come down. Two carpenters answered. They had a layover for a few weeks between jobs, and Lori put them up in the guest room. All meals were supplied, poor as they were. The carpenters rebuilt the Artley's roof but admitted that they had no idea of how to hurricane-proof it.

There was only one grocery store still open on the island, and that was because the owner stationed several young family members up on the roof holding shot guns. They never had to fire a shot. Looters were all over the island stealing anything on which they could get their hands. When they came into the plaza and spotted shotguns up on the roof, they stopped short and went elsewhere. Due to this, the plaza was the only place that anything could be bought for a long time. Other than the plaza, all the stores on the island had been looted, even doors and walls torn down by the "aborigines". If the hurricane didn't get the stores, the looters did.

Although three hurricanes have come by since, the Artleys have had no more damage except to the garden which was inadvertently rearranged. Other houses on the island, even some that Hugo never touched, were damaged or demolished by the next three hurricanes. If a hurricane wants, a hurricane gets.

No phones were connected til Christmas. Even then some residents didn't get them back til June. Hugo came in September! The phone company did install several phone boxes at various spots on the island and there were long lines for the use of them. Lori and Bill phoned their two children living in the states assuring them and telling them not to worry.

Many cars had been damaged and cracked windshields or taped up windows were usual sights on the roads. Bill had taken care to park their cars far from any trees and they discovered that their driveway in back was shielded by the cliff beside it. Hardly any turbulence occurred there. Even a basket-weave table left on the patio had never been moved from that spot.

After Hugo, almost every mechanical device needed a little help from oil. The moist, salty air along with sand and debris fouled up more mechanisms than will ever be known. The flying nails and cactus-needles on the roads punctured tires as if the dislodged roof tops and tree-blocked roads had not made transportation already more than impossible. Walking was the best way to get to some places. It was also difficult to find a service station that was open to sell gasoline or fix tires. Every able bodied person was making big money at construction.

Cash was scarce and places that had always taken checks before didn't take them now. Bill had always dealt with the S & S gas station, and the owner was a "life saver" by cashing his checks now, as all the banks were closed. Any people who came up to their house to help expected to be paid in cash. They had to have it to rebuild. It was needed to survive.

All around the island the boats had been carried inland, torn apart or sunk. Some masts were sticking out of the water so the owners could salvage them before they rotted.

Sporadically the sun would shine through the holes in the roof and Lori noticed how light it made their dark kitchen. While buying new windows in a shop, she noticed they had three sky lights for sale. After inquiring about them, the salesman said two matched and the third was a different kind. In a split-second decision, Lori said "That's O.K. because I am going to put two in the kitchen and one in the bathroom". That was such an improvement to her dark teak wood kitchen that she went on to putting up a white canvas ceiling and finally antiquing the dark brown cabinet doors with off-white to complete the evolution. The hurricane helped to show her the way to a light, airy kitchen. "It's an ill wind that carries no good."

Due to all this stress, Lori developed a rash of brown dots on her upper left arm. The itching kept her from sleeping at night. She used to pray, "Dear God. I don't need anything more right now. My burden is already all I can bear".

She went to three different dermatologists to cure it, and none of them could, saying that it was due to the stress of the hurricane. Finally, nine years later, Lori had skin cancer on her nose and was using Efudex to get rid of it. Since it worked on her nose, she checked out this wonder drug on her rash. After about three months of putting it on once a day, the rash disappeared. Miracles of miracles! Finally.

Dawn and Chuck came down at Christmas and painted the whole inside of the house. What a relief to be rid of all the little green and brown remnants of the many plants that had been on the island before Hugo. Two weeks after the hurricane, they noticed tiny snatches of green stems coming up from the rain soaked soil. Then little papaya trees soon appeared all over the land from seeds scattered by the winds. Then the yellow birds, and the iridescent humming birds and the big, bold Caribbean mocking birds came back. Out of the Artley's windows they could hear bees buzzing into each flower humming "slurp, slurp, slurp" as they sucked the nectar, and they forgot about Hugo.

Some disabled boats stayed on the land for six years or more, too damaged to repair. All the piers and boardwalks along the water were completely gone or totally damaged beyond repair. Years later the government finally built a new pier for the cruise ships and Navy, as the old one was unsafe. But the old one was fine for scuba divers who came from around the world to see the nesting places of the sea horses, lobsters and other organisms. The local government insisted on tearing up the old piles, loading them on barges where they dried for two weeks, and then towing them to a bay which was 60 feet deeper. There they were dumped. Any organisms still left alive could not survive at that depth. Lori wondered, "Why didn't they leave them alone and just build the new pier some distance away?"

Another waste of time for which some members of the legislature were well known, was when they denounced the merchants of the city for rebuilding the preexisting boardwalk along the water's edge. They wanted to force them into tearing it down and then applying for a permit to rebuild it. Then, if it ever got approved, the merchants would again have to pay for it being rebuilt. This was "government in action"!

The Red Cross counted 3000 buildings there which disappeared from the earth during Hugo, but this did not even include the many separate apartments and condominiums in which people lived inside those buildings. Beside that over 9000 buildings, like the Artley's home, were damaged. This of course left a housing shortage. While many people, especially children, left the island, the skilled construction workers from all over the world came in. In the Artley's 1-person apartment on their lower level, three construction workers bunked by their own insistence. They slept in sleeping bags. They were wonderful tenants...always ready to help and required little personal amenities. Also, they always paid the rent on time.

Others who were not so fortunate as to have a roof over their heads slept on the beach or in old, discarded cars...wherever. But they restored St. Ursula Island and they' re remembered and loved by all.

A great building boom ensued. Many home owners also built small houses on their extra land to rent out to these construction workers or dislocated islanders. Others bought up the hurricane damaged homes cheaply and renovated them, selling them at a tremendous profit. The federal government sent in 400 trailers for the homeless, and then the thankless people complained that the roads through their trailer parks were not paved and it made dust in their rooms. For $35.00 rent per month, they demanded paved roads!

Islanders had to get used to searching for bottled water, food, candles, hardware, medicines, furniture and even ice. After a month the Insular Superintendent of Schools forced all teachers to go back to work even though neither houses nor schools were yet secured. The Artleys' outdoor dogs could walk into the house at any time as there were no doors. The private schools had used makeshift rooms to open, and so, this pressured the public schools to open also.

Each day Lori and Bill went to work with trepidation. Fear that their house might be looted while they were gone hovered over them. No one was guarding the house but the dogs and their guardian angels. Their power prevailed.

After school some days, Ms. Angel and Mrs. Artley would drive in search of the free food FEMA was distributing. Being a native, Ms. Angel knew how to get to all the secluded distribution centers, but the only trouble was that many of the foods they gave out were not good for most people to eat. Vienna sausages and pork may be a delicacy, but they were not on Lori's high cholesterol diet.

As teachers, they were forced to get to school each day at 7:00 A.M. as the schools were now on double sessions. The penalty was being fired. Since both Bill and Lori had to be out of the house at the same time, and still weren't able to find any sliding glass doors to replace their broken ones, they decided to secure the house with steel grills made to fit all the openings. Grills came quicker and were more secure than the glass doors. The glass store was only filling the orders for commercial buildings and "holding" the home orders as they were "less important". Ever since the night of the hurricane, their dogs liked being in the house so they went in anytime a door was open. With the grills on at last the two big, outdoor dogs had to stay out in the tropical air.

At school, faculty and students alike were demoralized by the devastation. There was no drinking water, so everyone was supposed to bring it individually. But what if the students had not enough portable thermos' for their whole family? The toilets were all broken except the one in the main office, so the school administration didn't worry about that. That was the one they used! The students used the outer school toilets even though they did not flush which caused the consternation of the custodians. Toilet tissue had never been provided and they were constantly out of cleaning supplies. "Bring your own", was the cry.

There was no school library for the students to use as the books Mr. Svenske had saved from the storm were still packed in boxes. The head librarian, Mrs. History had lost her entire house plus most of the school library. She was a basket case. They all were! It was heartening for Lori to see Mrs. History regain her zest for living when she finally was able to rebuild her house. She asked Lori to recommend some paintings for her walls. Mrs. History finally rebuilt her house and the school library, too, including two new computers to catalogue the 6000 new books the federal government sent. Mrs. Artley asked Mrs. History, "Where would we have been without the good old U.S.A.?"

All the teachers, staff, and administration seemed to be doing their routine work by rote. The remaining 50% of the students were like zombies. They couldn't care less whether they did their school work or not. The other 50% of the students had been sent to relatives.

It was difficult to motivate those post-hurricane students but once in a while there would be a "shining light" among them who made coming to work each day worthwhile.

Lori's classroom was at the opposite end from the Art Department. It was made of dark gray cracked cement blocks and had all the electrical wires hanging down to the right height for hitting the heads of the students. It was a good thing there was still no electricity! For Lori, the depressing dimness of the classrooms without electricity was the worst thing about teaching that year.

In the reparation of the school, the local government built three cement block houses along the school fence. These supposedly would house future generators for emergency use. The only problem was they had no doors on the openings and they had no generators ever put in them but the block houses were still sitting there, waiting.

After a year the roofs and the classrooms were finally repaired at Central. Lori was asked to paint numbers on the new classrooms so teachers and students would know their rooms the following September. Fortunately Lori had stencils donated by Ms. Witch, a generous teacher who had no use for them. The principal had tried to buy stick-on numbers, but found that he couldn't get enough zeros to mark all the rooms. It was a good thing because they would have either fallen or been pulled off by those wanting a "trophy." The stenciled room numbers still remained to this day as they were painted on the wall. Behind each number, Lori had painted a white square so future student painters could use a roller to skip that area without obliterating the numbers.

Figure 9

Aftermath

Finally the school had just recovered from Hugo, when along came hurricane Marilyn. Even though Marilyn was only half the strength of Hugo, all the damage that was incurred to Central High was still not repaired by the following hurricane season. The tarpaulins were still on the roofs and the library was again unable to be used for the entire school year. After just getting finished repairing from Hugo, it seemed they just gave up on Marilyn!

When Lori read about other schools all over the globe, she found that many of them NEVER have any electricity ever. One article in the newspaper told of the deplorable conditions in Mexico where broken windows went unfixed, burned out lights were unreplaced, students cleaned the bathrooms and to obtain chalk, parents had to take up collections. The teacher's salaries were so low they couldn't even afford food. How counter-productive!

Lori knew that here on this island new teachers had to receive food stamps because they weren't paid until six months after they were hired, due to the archaic bookkeeping system. The government tried NOT to pay salaries or for supplies, thinking that it was saving money. They harvested the interest on the money in the meantime! Businesses refused to have anything to do with the government once they wised up to the system of non-payment. After the hurricane one of the senators bought $7000.00 worth of emergency food from a local grocery store for the hungry people. The bill still hadn't been paid despite the emergency forms that were signed at the time. No business could survive with such a system.

Somehow it was easier to adjust to adverse conditions when Lori realized that things were worse elsewhere. Lori felt, "they'd better appreciate the good things they have, and in this case it was that St. Ursula Island was a United States Territory. The federal government sent in help in every form and with their assistance the island was rebuilt even stronger than before. Many people still wanted even more."

Since Central's gymnasium had been demolished, one of the senators made them rebuild it so it was ready for graduation that same year. Otherwise they couldn't hold graduation as that was the only place big enough to hold it.

Sadly, a nearby private school also had its gymnasium destroyed by Hugo, but that still hadn't been replaced. That gym also doubled as a cafeteria at lunchtime, so those students had no place for a lunchroom either...and nobody had the money to rebuild it.

Practically everyone who applied to FEMA had good reason but they were told to FIRST apply for a Small Business Loan. Even when their ability to repay the loan was not feasible (due to Social Security or disability), the SBA accepted them so the people could not get a FEMA grant. The people didn't want to go into debt so they did without.

The main thing about education is, Lori learned, if the students WANT to learn, they CAN LEARN, regardless of the deplorable conditions and seeming indifference.

The year after Hugo, the superintendent of schools appointed Ms. Grievous, a former teacher (now supervisor) to create a book about the hurricane with contributions from the students. The English teachers got the school children to write compositions which would express their inner feelings. Hopefully it relieved the stress that could be building up inside them. Mrs. Artley's Graphic Arts class made scratchboard drawings of the night of the hurricane. All of them turned out well. The black background with white line drawings were an excellent medium to express that night. When Lori took them over, she learned that they were the only drawings submitted and that Ms. Grievous couldn't decide which compositions to include. Lori suggested that she choose excerpts from each to avoid the repetition, as there were so many. Ms. Grievous thought this was an excellent idea. The book didn't get published until a couple of years later and publication was so scant that only the principals of each school received one, not the children who contributed. She did offer to mail them to Lori's students who had contributed, but by then all the addresses had been changed. Most had graduated and gone to the states for college or wherever. Some catharsis that was! Ms. Grievous was really pushing the "PULL" door, again.

4

THE ELITE

(or the Administration)

Living through eight different principals wasn't easy. Lori's first principal was encountered when she was twenty-one years old back in New York State. She had not yet graduated from college, and was taking the last art course. Matilda, another student in the class, told her that she should apply for the job of art supervisor. It was November and the regular art supervisor was pregnant. " There were no other applicants for the job opening", she said. "You could do it." After much persuasion Lori did go in to apply and the job was hers. She had three schools of about 1000 students, per week.

At her "home" school, she formed an art club and the principal gave permission for them to hold popcorn sales as fund raisers. They canvassed the classes the day before and just made up a few more bags than the orders solicited. They made money. The club was a big success and had an art show at the end of the school year.

Two things that Mrs. Artley didn't like in that school were being asked to be the speaker at the PTA meeting and the principal's method of "rating" teachers at the end of the year. That was a necessary evil each year, but when principals did it, she felt they should delve into each teacher's activities, travels, likes and dislikes. This principal, Mr. Manly, filled out the whole form <u>before</u> teachers even came in for interviews. He read it to her, telling things that weren't true, such as whether or not she had traveled. For twenty-one years, she had traveled quite a bit, from Florida to Canada. He changed it. Since then, although Lori never considered herself a world traveler, she had visited most of the United States, Canada, Mexico and the islands of the Caribbean. "See America first!", the Artleys felt.

At another school there was a very pretty, stylish lady principal, Ms. Likit, who wore designer eyeglasses. On days when she wore "silver" jewelry, she wore her silver eyeglasses, and on the "gold" days, she had a gold pair, exactly matching. She always was very agreeable to anything Lori proposed, one of which was a huge oil painting of a young student after school. Afterwards Lori drove him home out in the farm country as the buses had long gone.

The supply cabinets were always well-stocked and everything organized as that school system had a former art teacher at the head of the Art Department. Ms. Sitze ordered what was needed. Lori learned how to take inventory at the end of the year and how to teach finger painting from her.

It was their goal to teach the grade school teachers how to incorporate art into their regular lessons. There were no discipline problems as the teachers stayed in the rooms and finished up the art lessons if they ran overtime.

Lori and the other art coordinators also wrote a mimeographed book for the teachers to use as reference. The teachers were very grateful that Mrs. Artley inquired in the fall what subjects would be covered, so that the art lessons would supplement the classwork. That is the only way to really teach, Lori felt. Everything must work together toward one goal. Everyone benefits.

The third principal, Mr. Shadow, she rarely saw. His school seemed to run without him. The other art teacher there, Ms. Oh taught the junior high level, and she really needed him. Ms. Oh must have had laryngitis at the end of each day. Lori could see the difference in art class without their teachers present. Then students tried to get away with everything!

There was no way she could get to know the names of the approximately 1000 students each week, but, with the grade teacher present, no one misbehaved. It was an excellent method of teaching both the students AND the grade teacher at the same time. Years later, when selling their house, Lori did substitute-teaching. Teachers were no longer present in the art classes so she devised a way to keep track of the student's names. When attendance was taken, she jotted down the number before each name on a quick sketch of the room. If anyone misbehaved during class, she could quickly cross-reference them for the teacher to deal with the next day. "How did you know my name?" the students constantly asked.

While the unruly classes of Ms. Oh really touched her heart, there was nothing Lori could do. Ms. Oh had seventh through ninth grades, and the students were more interested in attracting the opposite sex than in learning art.

Although Lori wouldn't receive her B.F.A. until the end of that year, the Superintendent of Schools in Endicott, N.Y. had hired her when she told him that teaching was really just common sense. The shortage of art supervisors that year may have had something to do with it also. Mrs. Artley must have been doing something right, however, as they kept her on the next year til she and Bill moved.

The next principal was Mr. Treacher in a 7th grade school in Berea, Ohio. Lori was glad to be pregnant with their first child that year as it gave her a reason to leave in mid-year. The winters were so damp and cold in that area that even people who had never had sinus before, experienced it when they lived there. That winter Lori had sinus problems PLUS laryngitis in a school with only seventh graders!

They had newly renovated an old school and thinking he was doing right, the architect had placed the display boards up near the top of the wall in the art room. To put up student work, Lori had to stand on top of the cabinets on a chair. The students were too short to reach and the precarious perch might have been hazardous to their well being. Also, they balanced out the student schedules by alternating art with gym, so that some days Mrs. Artley had 40 girls, which were delightful. Other days she had 40 boys. The whole school had only seventh graders as they had so many that year. On the days the boys came, Lori turned up the record player, and gave them craft lessons. She thought, "they ought to put all the boys in a deep freezer for two years. When they thawed them out they would have not only matured to the mental age of the girls but also would know as much as they would have learned during that time."

On the day before Christmas, Lori felt feverish and had laryngitis. She went in, as she knew no substitute could hold the students when their spirits were so high. They were to make 3-dimensional Christmas trees on straightened coat hangers with torn green construction paper branches and would take it home for a decoration. It would have developed their sense of balance as well as honed their abilities to "tear" instead of cut. Unfortunately they took the trees with them but left the tearings from the alternating branches on the floor instead of in the waste basket. By the time they walked out the door, Lori's voice had disappeared, and she felt too sick to sweep the room. "Oh well", she thought, "the janitors will sweep all the rooms over the holidays". She was wrong. The janitors did not sweep that room and kept it, as it was, for Mr. Treacher to see when he came back from the holidays.

When she came in, he confronted her, and Mrs. Artley was happy to inform him that she would be leaving at the end of the month due to pregnancy.

He acted sorry, but they replaced her with a male teacher. Exactly what those boys needed! After she had her baby, the girls in the class stopped by with a baby gift. They had all missed each other. Lori retired from teaching until her growing family got older.

About ten years later, Lori and Bill found themselves in Hartford, Connecticut. Since their three children were all in school then, Lori decided to teach in the inner-city schools. They gave her three small emotionally-challenged schools plus some normal classes to fill her schedule. She visited them each week: one in the north end (which had mostly Afro-American students); one in the south end (which had mostly Puerto-Rican students); and one in the middle (which had mostly transient and foreign students). The three principals were all excellent, but the art supply cabinets were separate and unequal. Usually she had to carry a basket of art supplies from one school to the next so the supplies would be available for specific lessons. Lori was hired to teach only in the mornings, but it took all day to put away one group of supplies and get ready for the next day. While in Hartford, she was able to design an art inventory survey for the students which would show what projects they most enjoyed. It also showed enrollment went UP when it was art day. Students evidently made a special effort to come to school when something special was going on. They didn't come for "readin', 'ritin' and 'rithmetic" which they learned anyway, but they DID come to school on those days when they had band, chorus, driver education, physical education, drama, photography, music, or art.

"A word to the wise."

That study was evaluated and sent to Washington, D.C. with photographs. As far as Mrs. Artley ever knew, nothing further was done.

Feeling frustrated, her next teaching assignment was along one of the main arteries out of the city, to Bloomfield, where she was promoted to teaching high school art. The students were more serious and looking forward to graduation and being on their own. Motivation was easier. The principal, Dr. Maceral, was a small, tense, middle aged man who couldn't understand that if she taught art in two different rooms why she needed a cart to get the supplies back and forth. He said she could "requisition one for the following year". In the meantime she bought one herself, as she needed it THEN.

One day Dr. Maceral informed her that her classes would be moved in midyear to a half built school down the street along with the entire freshman class. This was being done to alleviate the over-crowding at the high school. They would be moved with NO art supplies as the two other teachers in the high school needed everything. What? No art supplies?

Mrs. Artley had to inform her classes what was in store for them. Evidently some students went home and told their parents and the next thing she knew was the principal called her into his office and asked for a list of all the art supplies she would need for the spring term.

They had a very productive spring term. Since most students in the art classes wanted to become interior designers when they graduated, they created Geodescic Dome homes and invented curved furnishings to fit. They learned how to gain privacy for the interior rooms; how to design new furniture; and how to build a 3-dimensional dome-home with oaktag circles mounted on a sheet of gridboard. Mrs. Artley mounted them all on the barren walls of the large art room. One outstanding girl, who was most serious about this project, went home and built a large, wooden dome-home and interior furnishings for it. The class could see inside through the open centers of the circles on the curved roof. It was magnificent.

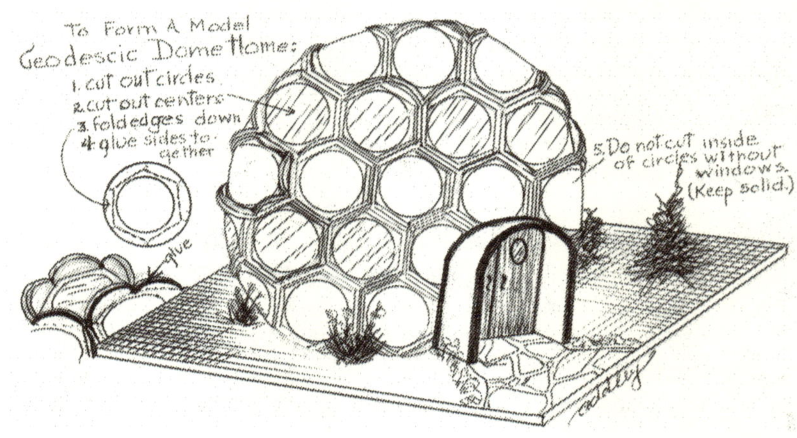

Another lasting project those classes contributed to the school was inspired by a set of famous Afro-American busts which were based on a pricey series which Seagram's had commissioned and advertised. These art classes made twenty-six sculptures using a Styrofoam base and a balloon head covered with colored tissue papier maché. Lori had driven down to a Styrofoam factory which gave, gratis, all the Styrofoam the car would hold, to school teachers who wrote to them. The students used typewriter ribbons for old-fashioned bow ties, wire for old-fashioned eye glass rims and dyed cotton for hair, beards and mustaches. Each was labeled with the name of the person, his or her accomplishments, and the student-artist's name at the bottom. They were donated to the school library, as in that elementary school, this was the only time that high school student-artists would be in that art room to create such sophisticated, realistic masterpieces. All twenty-six of them were first displayed on top of the shelves of books, but then later, the librarians concentrated on one per month.

When they held an openhouse for the new students who would be coming the following fall, a little Afro-American third grader was coming out of the library as Lori was walking by. Mrs. Artley heard her exclaim, "Gee, I like that library".

It made everything worthwhile! They were pushing the "PUSH" door, that time.

The fact that the majority of those students chose to become interior designers as a profession influenced Lori. The following year she left to become an interior designer herself. It sounded like more fun than teaching. The other teachers told her that she left at the right time. After she left, "came the deluge".

She enjoyed that profession for ten years, when Bill retired from the University of Hartford and they moved to the U.S. Virgin Islands.

On St. Ursula Island, the Artleys wanted to be part of the community and there was such a shortage of certified teachers, that it was natural that they both returned to educational fields.

Even though Mrs. Artley's principal there, Mr. Boss didn't always think so, she was very loyal to his policies. When the Legislature decided to charge $100 per student for taking the Driver Education course, which formerly had been free, the students got up a petition. They could readily get signatures in the cafeteria, and when it went to the Legislature and the local newspaper, the proposed fee was lowered to $50. Lori had no sooner gotten through collecting the $50 when the Legislature learned that the five-year-old cars could no longer be insured. They abruptly dropped the course in mid-term. The school chose not to refund the hard earned fees until AFTER graduation the following spring. Mr. Boss did not appreciate the whole sordid mess, but he seemed to have a premonition that this was coming. He had shunted Mrs. Artley over to teaching two art courses in order to free up Ms. Lash. She had been slated to become the Department Chairperson. Mrs. Artley also kept up the classroom phase of the Driver Ed class till the end of that term and finished the text book. Even if they could do no more driving, they got the best classroom course ever.

Soon after Lori arrived at Central, she volunteered to do drawings, signs and lettering reproduced for booklet covers for Mr. Boss. Because all loose signs "walked off", she suggested that they be painted directly on the wall. There they would stay until painted off when no longer needed. In the gymnasium she painted over thirty different signs including wordy warnings to would-be thieves. These were posted at both gates:

VIOLATION

VANDALISM OF THIS PROPERTY IS PUNISHABLE BY
MANDATORY SENTENCE: 2 YEAR IMPRISONMENT.
UNAUTHORIZED PRESENCE ON PROPERTY IS PUNISHABLE
BY MANDATORY MINIMUM SENTENCE OF 6 MONTHS
IMPRISONMENT.

The campus joke was: "Anyone who could read that sign, wouldn't have to steal for a living"!

Mr. Boss finally realized that he had done everything possible as a principal at Central, and decided to move "up the ladder". He gave notice and waited for an appointment. After a year in a job created for him as the Department of Education's "liaison" with the teacher's union, he was finally moved up to become the Assistant Commissioner of Education. Scuttlebutt was that his job as "liaison" called for having a beer once a month with the president of the teacher's union, and he still received his salary. Often it wasn't that simple.

Figure 70

"SIGNS OF THE TIMES"

There were several teacher's strikes throughout Lori's years at Central. Usually they marched down to Government House and speeches were given. Other times they carried placards and picketed the high school gates. Lori made many signs. The Union always sent lots of refreshments for the teachers and held parties at the end of each school year. Sometimes they negotiated contracts with the governor's representative. After, he signed and they all went back to work. Governor Fairweather reneged. Finally the case went to court and the teachers won, but the governor said there was no money in the treasury. Almost always the government owed the teachers money, which occasionally came years later in retroactive pay with interest right before elections. The government often gave lip service to "Education: our highest priority" but paying for it was their lowest priority. All the islanders were happy to see Governor Fairweather go, after the elections.

In a world where one gets what one pays for, Lori felt, their youths could not have been very important. Sometime over the following summer, half of all the money deposited by each department and club in the general fund, disappeared. The general fund was supposedly to keep the money "safe" but it turned out that it was the principal's prerogative to use, at his discretion, up to half that money. Mr. Boss left and in the fall, a new principal appeared on the scene.

Mr. Buffalo-soldier, a former Phys. Ed. teacher and then vice principal at Central, was now principal. Before coming there he had been in the armed forces and decorated his office with framed certificates to prove it. He played favorites, especially former service men and spent his free time shooting basket ball with his chums in the gym. The only thing Mrs. Artley had in common with him was that both had the same bunion bone operation.

Lori's operation was years ago while his was as principal and he had trouble walking. Knowing the pain, she sympathized. Because of her operation, she had brought a doctor's note to excuse her from wearing the mandatory closed-toe shoes.

Mr. Buffalo-soldier ran the school like the army and referred to the campus as "THEIR" campus, while his office was "HIS". He stayed in his office a lot. One peculiar thing about the office was one could NEVER have a confidential conference. Other people kept coming in and doing things or the principal would be calling people on the phone or reading his mail while conferences were supposedly going on. There was no such thing as privacy with any of the principals.

Figure 11

"CHANGING OF THE GUARD"

Trying to complete all the things he asked of Lori, such as handing in reports and making signs, she could not help but resent seeing her signs up in other schools around the island. He evidently offered her services to other principals as if she were being paid for the jobs. Many times she had to use her own materials as the ones he thought he had were not available anymore. Also he presented some signs as RUSH jobs, to keep students from being injured on the old bleachers before tearing them down. It turned out they couldn't find the proper hardware to put the signs up, so it was four months that the students had to keep themselves from being injured there. Lori wondered," What would have happened if any students had been injured during that time?"

Mr. Buffalo-soldier went off for summer vacation finally, leaving all the things that were needing repair to "others". When nothing was done by the end of August, the Superintendent of Schools replaced him. It was rumored that there were four people on the education payroll that year who had no positions. He was one of them.

One morning after a tumultuous rain, Lori woke up and turned on the radio to hear that all schools would be closed for the day. When such great rain storms came, school buses were unable to pick up the students and many teachers could not get through the water-filled potholes. This was the only school Mrs. Artley ever knew which closed for rain, but for good reason. When ever it rained while the students were at Central, the clay soil turned into "slip" when wet and everyone would slide and fall into the mud and puddles.

Sometimes the students would congregate under the portico of a building during the rain, as there were no covered walkways to their classes. One would pay another student to "fall" into the muddy estuaries which formed in the hollows all over campus. Then all the students would laugh, but the student who did it got to leave for home early and though the clothing was wet, the pockets were jingling.

On her way to Central, Lori had to cross a riverlet activated by the sudden rain and diverted across the road, sometimes flooding nearby houses. This was one of those days, and sure enough, the radio said that Central would be closed. Then she turned off the radio as numerous others did that day. Shortly after that, the "top banana" who was substituting for the Insular Superintendent called into the radio station saying that there WAS school that day. But most of the audience had turned off their radios and were getting some more shut-eye on that rainy, gray morning. Hardly anyone made it to classes that day. The cartoon in the local paper the next day showed the school administration in scuba gear behind their desks. Nevertheless, when the Insular Superintendent came back, she upheld that erroneous decision, docking the teacher's pay for the day, regardless of all the letters and cartoons that filled the newspaper. At the end of the week the final blow came in that fiasco when all of the teachers received a letter from the Insular Superintendent thanking them for the wonderful job they were doing. It was "Thank A Teacher" week!

Mr. Buffalo-soldier was replaced by a former vice-principal, who had also taught music: Mr. Teddybear. Almost everybody loved him. Dr. Mountain was one of his most dependable vice-principals and at his own retirement party Dr. Mountain told this story: "At one time he asked Mr. Teddybear if he thought of Dr. Mountain as his "private secretary". Mr. Teddybear replied, "yes".

Yes, Dr. Mountain was his right-hand man. He and everyone else tried to be of help except for two other vice-principals, who made themselves scarce to avoid extra work. "Were they jealous of him, or did they just have "teacher burn out"? Lori wondered. Somehow Mr. Teddybear survived the first year and the school became conditionally accredited under him. Even though all the teachers figured about three million dollars were needed to fix up the school, the government allotted a small amount of that to do some "cosmetic" changes in hopes that would "pass". Mr. Teddybear always threatened that he would be asked to leave because of the "hard time" he always gave the Department.

The only hard time he gave Mrs. Artley was when she was chairperson of the Fine Arts Department and he insisted that she should clean up the Art Office because it looked like a storage room. IT WAS A STORAGE ROOM! They had no place to store things, so had to store them in there. Also, it was needed to keep food students brought in to sell for the benefit of the band, when it had a fund raiser. Sometimes it was used as a classroom, when the chorus room was under water, and the class was small enough to fit. Lori used the three plywood sheets she had brought for table tops, to be made into shelves by the wood working department. On these, she could achieve some semblance of order in storing the colored construction paper and poster boards. She made a bulletin board of burlap and moved a file cabinet in there to file things neatly. They had a work table there which one of the teachers, Mr. Truck, carved up by cutting mats for student works. He neglected to use any padding or newspapers under his knife. And there was the phone, gotten illegally. It was supposed to go in the office next door, but since the door was locked and the Art Office wasn't, the telephone man was talked into putting it in the Art Office (by Lori). There were also a few chairs, a desk, a ditto machine and a small lithographed wood refrigerator. They did their best. It wasn't a Martha Stewart design.

After Lori retired, Mr. Hotshot, the new department head, removed the sets of shelves to use in his <u>own</u> room, and the paper was all over the place. It really looked like a hurricane hit it. Did Mr. Teddybear bug Mr. Hotshot, as he did Mrs. Artley? Of course not!

When Mrs. Artley announced she was retiring after ten years at Central, Mr. Teddybear threatened that he would hold a big retirement party to celebrate. Though she told him she wouldn't come, he insisted as Dr. Mountain was also retiring at that time. They didn't know that the only form of entertainment Mr. Teddybear knew was to hold a "roast". Even the teacher in charge of the arrangements, Ms. Twiggy, didn't know. If they all had known, they would have stayed home.

Mr. Teddybear required each vice principal to tell some half-truths about each of them, so they couldn't really deny it even though it didn't happen that way. When they had a chance for rebuttal explaining the truth would take too long so Lori only warned their fellow teachers, "not to believe a word of it". Then they presented Lori with a large, handsome, Chinese vase in copper and jade, which took over a corner of her living room.

The Art Department also had a private luncheon for Lori overlooking the ocean in a luxury hotel. They presented her with a beautiful collectible paperweight of clear glass mixed with the blues of the Caribbean ocean. Everytime she saw it in her home she thought of the crazy nuts from the Fine Arts Department at Central. They were always doing so many positive things for the school image in the community, but were never fully appreciated by the administration. Mr. Teddybear even said that since the Fine Arts Department was the smallest in the school, it should have the smallest budget.

Dr. Mountain, as the principal's right hand man, finally grew tired of nobody ever knowing the <u>exact</u> daily attendance of the students at Central High. Though originally built to house 1000 students, the enrollment was now between 2000 to 2500 each day but nobody knew exactly what that number was.

The attendance was supposed to be taken during homeroom each day, and sent to the office by the third period. The Daily Bulletin, which sometimes was published once a week, was usually full of errors but was supposed to be read to the class during homeroom. Most teachers just stuck a paper on the door on which the students would sign each other in; they never got to see the Daily Bulletin. The teachers could not be found but there seemed to be no penalty for the absence of anyone. Consequently, the daily attendance was hardly accurate. Homeroom had no "clout"! Students relied on their friends to give them the news or to sign them in, even when sick at home. Both the friends and the Daily Bulletin were not reliable sources.

In Mrs. Artley's room, the Daily Bulletins were displayed on the wall so students could come in and index back several weeks when they were looking to verify terms. Students she had never seen before came in as if it were the only place available.

The accurate attendance was a challenge to Dr. Mountain, who owned a personal computer and was the only person who had the guts to tackle the problem. Using student helpers, he worked out a method by which a student's name was listed alphabetically along with which classes s/he hadn't attended on a given day. It was obvious to the teachers that a class was "cut" if the student attended any other class that day. These cuts were printed out in a book of about twenty-six pages for each teacher each day. This print-out was indeed an eye-opener for the teachers as well as the students who had been cutting.

The only problem was that it took too much paper and the volunteer students who did the work were undependable every day. Dr. Mountain had no time to attend to any of the other duties expected of a vice principal. It did show that the computer method could work and for three days the attendance at Central was known.

Lori felt that attaching homeroom to the first period would make it possible to print the absentees the same day. It finally would have some "clout". Those who came late or didn't have a first period class, would have to go to the office for a pass, and thereby get counted.

Mr. Lackley was the vice principal mainly for the Vocational students at Central. Aside from asking Mrs. Artley to make banners for the science fairs, she rarely saw him. One time she recalled him talking loudly to a student in the hall. The student wanted to pay for a book which had been stolen, but Mr. Lackley refused, telling him, "I only collect money second period in my office". The student had a class that period and didn't see how he could get there at that time. He didn't know how he could do without his book, either, but that was Mr. Lackley's way of "toughening up" the students.

On the other side of the campus was another one of the vice principals, Mr. Past, who was also "the keeper of the keys". Mrs. Artley always felt that Mr. Lackley would have been more suitable for that job, as he was more mechanically minded and would have spent more time keeping track of them.

Mr. Past rarely had any keys to any rooms, except over the summer when the keys were supposed to be labeled and turned in. What a jumble they were stuffed into one large, brown paper envelope!

When a new teacher came, s/he had to rely on the compassion of fellow teachers to lend a key to take to the locksmith for a duplicate to be made. Many times new teachers had classes in several different rooms. If there were no keys, then nothing could be left in those rooms until new keys were made. If the building were new, then keys would be given out, but otherwise the administration took no responsibility for supplying a key. Yet, it was expected that the teachers should turn in all keys at the end of the year with no remuneration. Over the years the amount spent for keys yearly added up and no thought was ever given to see that each teacher received the use of the same room the following year.

For instance, after the Fine Arts Building was burned down, the two band leaders were shuffled around like a compost pile. Finally they were put in the gym on the second floor. Using their own funds for acoustical tiles, keys and labor, they managed to sound-proof that room and make it as usable as possible by June. At the end of the summer, they found that they were being scheduled for <u>another</u> room, after all the work they had done. There was no consideration of their needs in teaching band. Yet they were expected to produce a band to play for graduation each June. One of them quit then and there, and the other retired.

Lori wondered why the administration didn't make up a master-set over the summer, so that they could get into a room when the teacher was not present. Things would happen showing how little the administration "felt" for the faculty.

Within each class room, the locked closets or boxes for securing books were usually bought and built by the teachers. Even some doors to classrooms could easily be opened with a plastic card and the supplies would "walk" off. They couldn't even keep toilet paper in the lavatories as someone would "t'ief" it.

Because of this need for locks that worked, Lori offered, gratis, to engrave the number of each room into each key, over the summer vacation. After starting the project, she found that many departments just handed in all their keys on a ring unmarked. There was just one big bunch of keys marked "Spanish Department" or "Home Ec". Some rooms had so many cabinets with keys that she didn't know what to engrave on them.

She bought ten folders of ten pockets each; one for each tier of ten classrooms, and attached each key to an index card with a paper clip. Lettering the outside of each plastic folder, she numbered the pockets inside the folder for each room in that tier, and paper clipped the key onto the pocket with its index card. The plan was that when each key was signed out by the receiving teacher on the index card, the card would be re-clipped on that pocket with the room number on it. The system could have worked!

Early the following fall, Lori saw that it wouldn't when she observed Mr. Past giving out a key to a teacher WITH the index card, saying "Here's the card with it. When you fill it out, send it into the office." Even if the teacher ever did fill out the card and send it in to the office, no one in the office would know enough to put it in Mr. Past's mailbox. Why Mr. Past didn't have the teacher fill out the card BEFORE giving out the key, no one will ever know. The keys would have gotten organized. Lori could see that all her work had gone for naught.

Mr. Past sometimes "spread himself too thinly" even though he had the best of intentions. Not only was he a vice-principal in a school with lots of "vice", but he also was minister of his church, and had a growing family of five. Around school he was out of his office often. He was observed behind the door in the Registrar's Office where no one could reach him by phone. He undoubtedly had to protect himself from any more burdens being placed on his shoulders.

Ms. Sorority, another vice principal, was full of innovative ideas. When the class she sponsored was holding the prom, she always involved Mrs. Artley in handling the decorations. So that the Seniors could not say they couldn't afford to attend their own Prom, the Juniors always sponsored the dance. They did all the decorating, refreshments and acted as hostesses. It was usually held in the gym as that was the only place big enough on the island.

In order to afford this, the Junior homerooms were asked to either contribute or take part in a mini-carnival to be held in the gym. If each homeroom raised enough money, it would cover what each student was expected to pay.

Mrs. Artley's homeroom class chose to sell hot dogs and hamburgers and Lori had the duty of buying everything wholesale. Also, she later realized that they would need cooking pots, stoves, microwaves and all the other things needed to serve.

Unfortunately, the microwave was the probable cause for the fuses to blow as the circuits in the gym were not made to handle such a load. This happened toward the end of the mini-carnival just when the exodus of the participants would have paid for their costs by buying all those hotdogs and hamburgers on their way out. No electricity! Nobody even knew where the fuses were. It was chaos in the gym. Lori's homeroom had all those uncooked hamburgers and hotdogs left, plus buns, ketchup, relish, mustard ...and empty coffers.

The students had tried to keep accurate records, but with certain ones doing the bookkeeping, it turned out that there was no profit in the venture.

Mrs. Artley put the uncooked meat in her freezer until the following week. She brought in her big electric frying pan so she and some of the homeroom members cooked the rest of the food outside the R.O.T.C. building. R.O.T.C. generously allowed them to run an electric line through a window, and the buyers came when they smelled delicious cooking odors.

Even Ms. Sorority sent someone down from her office to buy her a hamburger for lunch. They couldn't cook fast enough.

After that sale, they were trying to figure out how much they should have made, when it became apparent that the profits were not there. Lori contributed the difference so that the homeroom paid their share. She decided then and there, that was the last time she would ever take part in that kind of fiasco.

In bookkeeping, they were definitely pushing the "PULL" door.

5

THE STAFF OF LIFE

(The Munching Moochers)

After reading the rule book, Mrs. Artley learned that the clerk-typists were supposed to type exams for the teachers. An experienced colleague clued her in, saying, "You had better do your own typing as they are known for the many mistakes they make".

As the years rolled by, Lori was glad she followed that advice. Nobody seemed to proof read anything on almost all the typewritten epistles which emanated from that office. If they did they didn't seem to know that plural words usually had "s" at the end. Instead of working, the typists spent most of the day spouting off about how much work they had to do, as they continually munched on junk food at their desks.

As time went on, Lori heard that the most obnoxious clerk-typist had been placed in that job by a certain Senator Chart. It was Ms. Grumbles, his relative, as it seemed every native on the island was related somehow to every other native. Ms. Grumbles did as little work as possible, usually very poorly, and muttering disgustingly all the time. She could never be fired and she knew it.

Ms. Grumbles was in charge of the school files, so when letters of displeasure about her poor performance or her undermining the morale of both students and faculty were received, she filed them promptly in the circular file beneath her desk—never to be seen again.

Another responsibility she had was keeper of the various forms for injuries and Workman's Compensation. Her file drawers were in such disarray that when she was absent, the other secretaries could not find those necessary forms. Injured students or teachers could not go to the Emergency Room without them. Lori felt it would be a life-saving move if these forms could have been kept in the nurse's office. Alas, Ms. Grumbles would feel that some of her power was being taken from her and the nurses would see this as "extra work".

One example of Ms. Grumbles demoralizing effect on Central was her refusal to answer any teacher's simple "yes" or "no" questions after 3:15 P.M. She didn't seem to realize that she and all school personnel were paid for a forty hour week, and she was "on duty" for eight hours each day, the same as everyone else.

Another time she was curt to a student who Lori had sent over with a "dolly" to bring back art supplies which had arrived from the warehouse. Disorganized as she usually was, she screamed at him that she was "too busy", and sent him back empty. Lori had to come over herself after school and load the heavy supplies onto the dolly, then cart them back and unload them, since the students had been dismissed by then.

The private secretary to the principal was Ms. Curt. In reality she was not very private. She would "tell all" to any interested parties as a show of power. On realizing this, the principal openly admitted that he had to type all his own letters if he wanted the subject of them kept private. Usually, nothing was kept very private in that office. Whenever anyone came in to speak to the principal, privately, people were coming in and out of his office the whole time, to do Xeroxing, faxes or find something in his files.

Ms. Curt unhesitatingly asked Mrs. Artley to make several personal signs for her use, which Lori did as a favor. Then at other times, Ms. Curt would blatantly say, "I'm not speaking to you" or call Lori "White woman" instead of using her name. Mrs. Artley got used to this type of put downs unless something specific was wanted by them. It was reverse discrimination.

When Lori first came to Central, the main office was jammed with big fat welfare recipients on the "Workfare" program. They just sat there squashing the folding chairs and cluttering up the main office. They were supposed to be "working" but they just chattered away, munching and ignoring any parents or visitors that came to the counter. The office gave a very poor appearance, crowded, inefficient and noisy. Finally Principal Boss got rid of all the welfare women and Principal Teddybear had cubicles built for all the clerk-typists so that no one would see them munching away on junk food or not doing their work. At least their personal habits would not be on public view.

The only secretary who Lori ever saw doing any work was Ms. Juan. She also took night courses at the local college. Ms. Juan was trim, pretty, bright and had a sense of responsibility. Finally this was recognized and she was put in charge of counting all the money which came in for the General Fund. When she needed to do several crafts projects for her college courses, Lori was happy to help her, and whenever Lori needed help in the office, she sought out Ms. Juan. Ms. Juan held the office together as she was usually the only one who pushed the PUSH door.

(The Mailbox Episode)

Most of the time at Central nobody answered the phone. The receptionist was never at her desk as she also sorted the mail, distributed the paychecks and went to the ladies room as much as possible. The phone would ring and ring. Sometimes a passing student would answer it or a guidance counselor would come out of her office to answer if the callers were lucky. Other times they just took the phone off the hook. The school found it difficult to keep a receptionist as the job was either too stressful or the pay was too low.

The teachers gave up trying to call in if they would be late in the morning.

Ms. Hybiscus was a very talented base violinist and had been on various T.V. shows and contests. She saw to it that her daughter also learned to play the base violin, and talked the music teachers into carrying on with her base violin studies while in high school. The two of them performed throughout the island and were a tourist attraction. They were beautiful, talented natives and looked like sisters. No wonder Ms. Hybiscus did not care for the details of the job of a receptionist and mixed up phone numbers. Her mind was on learning the computer and being "discovered." Finally there was a teacher shortage and she was asked to fill in as a language teacher in Spanish...her second tongue.

In desperation, the school had hired Ms. Hybiscus as a receptionist although she turned out to be dyslexic also. There are many other jobs dyslexics can do, but this meant the phone numbers were almost always transposed so that calls could not be returned and when mail was put in teacher's mailboxes, it often got in the wrong box. Instead of putting envelopes in the box to the right of the number, she put them in the left. This meant that the teacher who received the erroneous message had to find out for whom it was, (as this was often omitted) and then redeposit it in the correct box. This box number had to be looked up on a posted sheet and sometimes this process took two weeks to occur.

Figure 82

"THE MAILBOX EPISODE"

A mixup such as this deprived Ms. Lash of half a day's pay, once. Since an accreditation meeting had been scheduled during the last period of the day, Ms. Lash had asked Mrs. Artley to be excused to supervise a student who was finishing up a painting due to his illnesses. It had to be finished that day, as the following day she had scheduled a test, and he wouldn't be elligible to take it if he didn't finish his painting. Since this was the first week of Mrs. Artley's duties as chairperson, she didn't know that she didn't have the authority to excuse Ms. Lash from the meeting, so Lori told her to go ahead. Mrs. Artley felt Ms. Lash was needed more in the classroom than at the accreditation meeting, as the Fine Arts Department was not reporting that day.

Ms. Lash was missed that day by Mr. Past who was taking attendance. Mr. Buffalo-soldier, the principal, docked her pay the following morning and advised her in writing. Ms. Hybiscus put his letter in the wrong mailbox and Ms. Lash didn't get it until two weeks later. By that time, he would not rescind his decision. No one knew who was the primary recipient of Mr. Buffalo-soldier's letter, but the teacher who had gotten it, opened and read it, probably taking it home and bringing it back but forgetting it a few days. Then it was put in Ms. Lash's mailbox after the number was looked up. What a comedy of errors!

After that, Lori spent an hour drawing arrows with a magic marker under each number, pointing to the 150 mailboxes. She realized that Ms. Hybiscus must no longer put the envelopes in the wrong boxes. It seemed peculiar to teachers who observed, but Lori knew it was necessary.

(Liming for a Living)

In the vernacular of the island, "liming" meant loitering or just standing around. That is what the school monitors were paid to do. Their mere presence made rambunctious students think twice before "acting up". When the daily fracases did occur, watchful eyes were there.

At Central, the ten long tiers housed ten 1-story classrooms each. The Fine Arts Building and the gymnasium stood above them with two-stories plus a 1-story cafeteria built to house about 1000 students. Later the Vocational Department was added with two more wings of buildings and the R.O.T.C. added their building to the campus. As the student body exploded into 2500 students temporary trailers gave Central additional classrooms, but what was really needed was another high school. There are other Central schools all over the world, some of which have three stories, two stories and enclosed campuses, unlike this open campus on St, Ursula, which boasted a Frank Lloyd Wright type design.

The problem with an open campus was lack of security. To control those going in and out, Central built a sturdy chain link fence around the perimeter, with paid monitors patrolling the campus. Ordinarily this could work except for those who would cut holes or break through the fence, allowing easy access for drug dealers and non- students as well as those who wished to leave before the final bell.

Figure 93

"THE FIGHTS"

Lori thought a better design for monitoring would be building one-story classrooms around the perimeter, attached, except for the gates in front and back. The center "green" could be used for fire drills and for picnic tables under shade trees. If ever more classrooms were needed, second stories could be built on top of the originals, using outdoor staircases.

Pebbles should not be used underfoot as certain dysfunctional students had a tendency to throw them at "cute chicks", so they would be noticed. They never realized that they could blind fellow students for life.

The window louvers should be small enough so that bodies couldn't slide through them. All of this would make less work for the monitors.

At this school, the monitors kept students away from the main hallway and ushered them over to the gym for assemblies. But after school and on weekends, the campus was deserted and vandalism and outright thefts resulted. Nowadays, many schools have a watchman living in a trailer on campus. Lori knew, thieves stay away when there was the possibility of being identified.

At Central, students often planned fights with each other, to get out of going to class. The paid adult monitors ought to have deterred them in this venture, but many times students had to try and outsmart them. Beside intervening in student fights, the monitors also presided over forced searches to find controlled substances or weapons in the possession of some students.

Notices such as this were sent out to the teachers so they would excuse surprize absences from class.

TO: FACULTY AND STAFF
NOTICE:
DATE: MARCH 5,

This morning, a search was conducted by monitors, with the help of police officers from the School Security Unit and Territorial Marshals. During this search, knives and other weapons/contraband were recovered.

We realize this may have been a bit inconveniencing; however, we must take action to address the problems facing our school. As always, our primary concern must be ensuring the safety of the entire student population, faculty and staff. This operation was but the first step toward addressing our problems. We will keep you informed of other measures in the near future.

Thank you for your cooperation in our efforts to improve our school.

Creating an "open campus" for any school below college level was building a "disaster-on-the-way-to-happening". Modifying the concept to avoid pitfalls would make a center of learning where students would enjoy an atmosphere which teaches things they will use all their lives. This is why Lori Artley went into teaching.

While the monitors were invaluable when the students were rioting or going berserk, most other times they were just standing around, supposedly "watching". Sometimes they were obnoxious.

One time Mr. Longjohn, one of the monitors, was moving chairs back into the rooms from which they were taken for some affair. He tried to push a metal folding chair, which was clearly marked with the number of another room, into Mrs. Artley's room. She had finally gotten rid of all those cold, metal chairs as the students felt uncomfortable in that freezing over-air-conditioned room. Now that she had secured enough plastic chairs, he was trying to put this one in her room. She tried to persuade him to put it in the room marked on the back, but he disagreed and got into a shouting match. One of the things he shouted, hysterically was, "Central doesn't need old, white teachers, like you".

He left the chair, which was put in the hall immediately. Lori lived to see him retract those angry words after she retired. Mr. Moresum, head monitor, phoned her at home saying she was missed at Central. She knew he wanted some favor, and it was the repainting of four outdoor signs which Mr. Hotshot's students had painted, with many errors. She corrected the refractions of the English language and sprayed them with clear acrylic spray paint, as outdoor paint had not been used on some parts. Mr. Longjohn was there when she brought the signs back and Mrs. Artley forced him to retract his previous statement. Central still needed "old, white teachers" like Mrs. Artley.

Another monitor, Mr. Bigbutt, found the lock on Lori's door broken, so he removed a chair on which to sit outside. He also left the door ajar so that students could also remove the hard earned chairs. As Mrs. Artley came back for her next class, she noted the room number on the backs and proceeded to confiscate the chairs and carry them back to her room. The last chair was the one on which Mr. Bigbutt was sitting.

Expecting another fight she approached him gingerly. Pointing to her room number on the back, she let him know that this chair was needed for her classes. No response. Finally he did get up, but held on to the chair. She pulled on the other half and finally freeing it from his grasp, carried it back to her room again. The watching students were delighted with the confrontation and gathered around to see who would win.

A short time later, Lori and Bill encountered Mr. Bigbutt moon-lighting at a local hotel dining room as a waiter. Changing his tune, he was the soul of good manners and solicitation. What an actor! She was now a "customer".

It was rumored that Mr. Moresum made unsolicited long distance phone calls from the phone in the Fine Arts Building, when the school was closed. As head monitor, he had keys to all the buildings. Someone had seen him. Since he moonlighted by doing promotional work for local shows, the rumor sounded plausible. Shortly afterward, he was relieved of his title.

While carrying paper supplies into the locked closet in the band room, some of the monitors played with the kettle drums and other instruments lying around. That locked closet was created for band instrument storage. The band needed it, but the school had appropriated it for bathroom tissue. Evidently the administration felt they were more important than the instruments.

While most of the male monitors looked like gangsters, the lady monitors blended in with the faculty, as well as a few of the men.

Outstanding was Mr. Khaki, one of the monitors and a retired military man. He often wore army fatigues and walked with a military bearing. At times it was frustrating for him but he continued to carry out his duties as a monitor as well as doing a lot of little extra things. When finally the monitors received Walkie Talkies in order to communicate with one another for back-up when necessary, Mrs. Artley thought she would be able to use the one Walkie Talkie which a houseguest had given her years ago. If she ever needed help, she would at last be able to call.

Figure 104

"THE SECURITY GUARD"

Lori dug it out at home and brought it in to Mr. Khaki, as she had never used it. Without any intercoms in the classrooms, there was no way to communicate with the outside world when the door was shut. Mr. Khaki tried to adjust it to the school frequency but determined that in spite of its forty channels, it must be on the wrong wave length to communicate with theirs.

In lieu of the unusable walkie talkie, Lori bought a plastic trigger bottle and put red Batik dye in it. It was "cabinet ready" for any invasion to her room. Several times she had need, and it enabled her to chase out uninvited marauders without calling the monitors. The student invaders ran when they saw it, as they could see it would dye their white shirts red, and the monitors would then haul them into the Principal's Office.

Another late afternoon when everyone had left, Mr. Khaki came walking by her car which wouldn't start. He determined that the fuel line was blocked. Some passing R.O.T.C. students pushed the car enough to get it going since it was a stick shift. She then drove to the nearest gas station. Without that help, she might still be there in that Central School parking lot.

At one period of time, a security company was hired at Central to curb vandalism. Lori saw one of them in the ladies lounge, slumping down in an easy chair with a portable T.V. perched on her fat stomach. After that company was discharged, it was found that there was less vandalism than while they were at Central.

A few minutes early for her second period class, Mrs. Artley found all the doors in the Fine Arts Building had their key holes stuffed with wet toilet paper. Mr. Kiley, one of the few nice monitors, tried to clean it out to no avail, so in desperation, he removed the hinges from one of the double doors to her art room, so the students could come in.

Using bent pins, hair pins and tools borrowed from the carpentry department didn't do the trick, so finally they had to call the locksmith to come on an emergency mission. He knew how to clean the locks so that the room could be secured before they left for the day.

Figure 15

CLEANING OUT THE DOOR LOCKS

All the money this mission cost the school could have been spent on something meaningful for the students rather than on a useless, student prank. Lori felt that those students who were not serious about learning would be better off in a trade school instead of deterring those who came to school to learn.

Figure 16

"THE ROCKS"

Mr. Kiley also helped Mrs. Artley when trying to chisel the school monogram into the large "blue bitch" stones at the entrance of the school. He seemed to lack the prejudice against "white's" which some of the others exhibited and he was always smiling and helpful to everyone. It was a joy to have SOME of the monitors not always pushing the "PULL" door.

One day the monitors arranged a "sting" operation to catch two students who were intimidating one of Mrs. Artley's students, Jorge. He told her that each day at lunch time, they forced him to give them his lunch money. The monitors arranged to have one monitor standing near Jorge but looking the other way, while a second monitor stood a distance away in the shadows but with her eyes never leaving Jorge.

Sure enough the predators approached Jorge and when he started to get his money out, the two monitors closed in. When those two students were prodded off to the principal's office, many students were relieved. They evidently had been intimidating half the campus.

Throughout Lori's ten years at Central, the monitors asked her to make wooden passes for visitors which could not be duplicated by undesirables who might want to enter the gates. She also made signs for them so that strangers in cars would know to stop at the guard house and sign in.

Mrs. Artley mixed a maroon color which could not be duplicated and used this to mark the passes, and had her Graphic Arts class do the lettering on wood. Unfortunately the fifteen passes became collector's items, since they had the school colors. Their disappearance caused the use of them to be discontinued. The visitors never gave them back.

(Dozing Domestics)

With students occupying classrooms every period of the day, no cleaning could be done during class time. The custodians would squash themselves onto folding chairs in the long outdoor hallways, moving their mouths all at the same time except for those who fell asleep in full sight of all those who passed. Sometimes when two of them talked together, neither was listening but both were shouting at the top of their lungs.

One day, Ms. Gusto, the only custodian ever seen working, came to Mrs. Artley crying. She told Lori that she was going home because the head custodian would not give her a mop bucket that day. They were always squabbling among themselves! The custodians for the upper campus would not cooperate with those on the lower side.

Figure 17

"DOZING DOMESTICS"

Mrs. Artley made her promise to stay there until she got back from the hardware store where she was going her lunch period. Knowing that all the vice principals would be away for lunch that period, Lori drove to the nearest hardware store and purchased the one mop bucket they had. At least Ms. Gusto could finish out her day's work and not get fired. It gave her time to "cool down" and it would suffice until she would have a regulation mop bucket the next day.

Ms. Gusto was the only custodian who never sat down in the hallway. Her rooms were the cleanest, and she even went outside, with broom and dustpan and picked up the "throwaways" on the grass. When the big agricultural fairs were held each year, she always was there selling snow cones from her old metal cooler which she had previously asked Lori to paint up to look "nice" "How does one make an old snow cone cooler look nice?" mused Lori.

At the beginning of the school year, Mr. Treetop would throw away all the student ceramics from the previous year which hadn't been picked up by the students who made them. Ms. Gusto and the rest of the custodians would go down to his room for anything and everything that was going to be thrown away. One year Mrs. Artley was sharing his ceramics room and they came while Mr. Treetop was out. She inadvertently let them take some items which Mr. Treetop knew the students wanted. When he told her, Lori went down to find the items. It was a challenge but she got them all back by the time the students came for them. Some of the student's ceramics were very professional and many were happy to have them in their homes or gardens.

Other times, Mrs. Artley took a couple of boxes of the unwanted ceramics around the campus. Mr. Khaki looked them over and said he'd like to have the whole lot to put in the Spanish Club Room, they looked so good. Sometimes Lori brought them up to the main office where the clerk-typists went wild over them. One would think it was Christmas.

After hurricane Hugo, politicians allowed burning of endless debris, carcinogenic and otherwise, right across the street from Central High. Gusty winds saw to it that the ashes were layered over all the school desks, cabinets and chairs. It was not only a dirty, unhealthful environment, but they were condemning their youths to long slow deaths exposing them to carcinogenic ashes. In twenty years, there would be few young people of this age group and it would be too late to do anything about it. If they didn't know or care about that, the teachers did!

The teachers gave the administration an ultimatum. They wanted professional cleaning personnel to clear each room in the school. There was to be no more burning in that area.

The burning practically stopped after that. Occasional fires mysteriously came alive at night and no one knew who started them. The Department of Education had the cleaning done by the regular school custodians, and Mrs. Artley and her fellow teachers took three days off to allow time for the "thorough cleaning". Nobody liked having the pay docked, but it was their money or their lives.

Figure 18

"THE FIREBURN"

The custodians demanded protective clothing and air masks. The administration suddenly discovered they had no keys for the rooms. The teachers came back ready for work and discovered nothing had been done.

Mrs. Artley noticed that her room had not been cleaned so she checked with Ms. Sorority who was in charge of the custodians. Ms. Sorority blushed through her brown skin and borrowed Lori's key just before a teacher's meeting which was about to commence.

When Mrs. Artley returned to her room after the meeting, she found that all her large sheets of colored paper had been thrown out. She would have had a heart attack then if she didn't have low blood pressure. The custodians said, "It was down in the dumpster". They all trekked down to see what condition the papers were in. Lori climbed into the dumpster and handed hundreds of dollars worth of colored paper and oaktag out, as the custodians carried it back to her room. This is what happens when a room is cleaned without prior notice.

As one of the custodians left with her arms full of paper she told another, "I told you this looked too good to be thrown out."

Just before another teacher's meeting, Ms. Lash had put an expensive watercolor painting dryer-rack and a seven foot shelved cabinet outside her room. She didn't want them, anymore. Mr. Treetop good naturedly said he'd drive them over to Mrs. Artley's room, as she wanted them. After the meeting, the three teachers converged on Ms. Lash's room when they found the items gone. Were they taken by thieves? Who else would have use for them? They ruled out trash collection because that usually took six months.

Ms. Lash and Mrs. Artley canvassed the campus. They couldn't believe their eyes when they saw them in one of the dumpsters with the doors laying on the ground next to it. Unbeknown to the teachers, the trash men were hired to clean up the campus that day. When the trash men had spotted the furniture, all the teachers were at the meeting, so using their own bad judgement, they hauled off the cabinets. When Lori related the story, they felt terrible. To make up for their dastardly deed, they picked up the two items and delivered them right into Mrs. Artley's room. The carpentry students made new and stronger doors and Mrs. Artley's students were glad to have a place to dry their paintings and store their art supplies. All's well that ends well.

Figure 19

IN THE TRASHBIN

On one of Mrs. Artley's visits to the school after her retirement the custodians mentioned that Mr. Teddybear had sent them a letter and they didn't have a clue as to why he was making them work until 5:00 P.M. when they had always left at 4:00. After checking with the principal, Lori learned that he had had complaints about their cleaning, or lack of it, and was giving them after-school time so they could do it efficiently. This was not really fair to the few custodians who DID clean thoroughly, like Ms. Gusto, but he did not differentiate.

CENTRAL HIGH SCHOOL

TELEPHONE:
FAX NO:

Principal

Assistant Principal

Assistant Principal

Assistant Principal

KNOWLEDGE IS POWER

Memorandum

To: Custodial Workers

From: Principal

Date: March 22,

Re: Working Hours **(Final Notice)**

On February 15, you were notified that effective March 4, . your working hour will be from 8:30am to 5:30pm, with duty free lunch hour from 1:30pm to 2:30pm. To date you have failed to comply with this work schedule. Failure to adhere to this schedule will result in your time and attendance adjusted biweekly.

You are also required to sign-in and sign-out daily. Attendance sheets are located in the main office.

Prior to leaving the campus daily a complete inspection of all your assigned rooms must be completed to ensure that all lights/fans are turned off, and all classrooms and offices are secured.

Figure 20

THE LETTER

Lori had noticed the pillar outside the main office on which two of her students had painted a large "TAKE A STAND AGAINST DRUGS" sign. It got dirtier and dirtier. No custodian felt that it was in her territory. Lori decided that she had to clean the sign herself, and came in on weekends to do so.

Lori reiterated to them what the principal had told her so they would "get with it". She had always been a friend to them, and even brought in magazines and catalogues they could read in the lounge.

When she continued bringing them in after retirement she noted that sometimes the same custodians would be sitting in the same chairs each month. Mrs. Artley couldn't help but say," Are you still in the same chair as last month?" and everyone would laugh. It looked like they hadn't moved. Like the rest of the school, they were always pushing the "PULL" door.

(At one time the custodians took a vote among themselves as to which of the teachers would win the "Ugliest Teacher" Contest. The three candidates they decided were Ms. Grumbles, Mr. Beachball and Ms. Feelbad. The hands-down winner was Ms. Feelbad. With her pear-shaped body, her dyed red hair in long braids and her brown, freckled puffy face...she was a winner.)

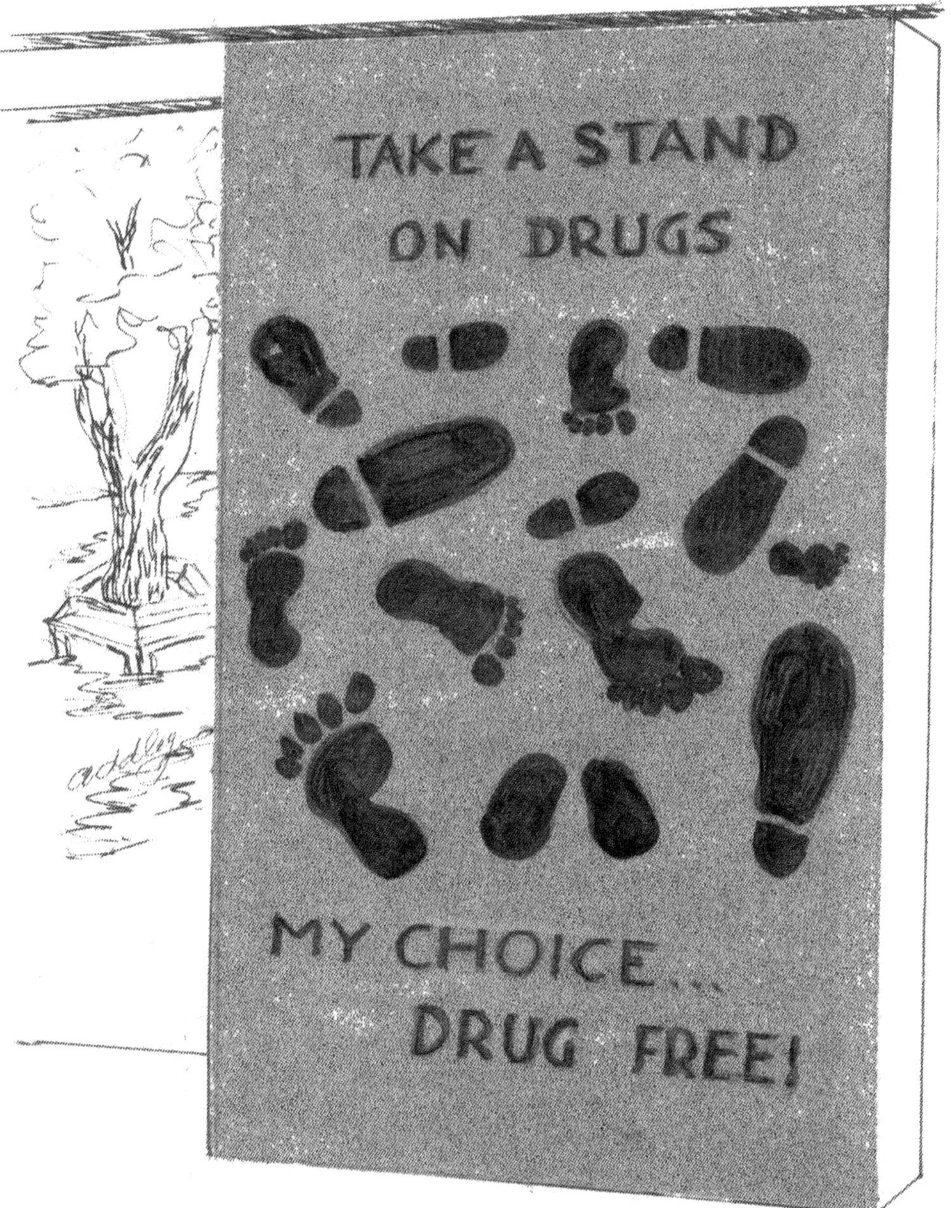

Figure 21

Drug Free Mural

(Ms. Peacock-feather)

The school registrar, Ms. Peacock-feather, a brown middle aged, spreading woman, never seemed to be doing any work but always bustled around, complaining of "so much to do". She was equally negligent about sending out transcripts for students wishing to enroll in other schools, as she was in keeping up their records at Central.

To a nearby private school, one Central student had applied for transfer. They couldn't accept him until they could see his records. In desperation they asked Lori, through her husband, Bill, who worked there, "Could she copy down his grades for the past three years and Bill would bring them in to the private school the next day?"

During her free period Mrs. Artley went down to the registrar's office, finding no one there except an open door and all the file cabinets full of records. While she was waiting for someone to come in and "man the office" she looked around at the file cabinets and found them marked for each grade. Lori pulled out the ninth grade drawer. Not one to waste time, she opened the folder with his name and jotted down his grades for the ninth grade. No one had come in yet, so she did the same with the tenth grade and 11th grade files. Still no one came back, so she left. She recopied the scribbles she had jotted down so they made sense and sent them with her husband. The registrar at the private school thanked her profusely and on the basis of her jottings, they decided whether to take that student or not. The private school never did receive anything from Ms. Peacock-feather. They would still be waiting for the grades, if it wasn't for Lori. At Central, if you wanted anything you had to do it yourself.

Another time the registrar's office sent out folders with three carbons for each page but no directions. Mrs. Artley gave them out to the students who came to her homeroom, but since there were three absent, she went to get extra pages for them in her free period.

At the Registrar's Office, no one answered her polite inquiry, though four people were standing in the same office, two engrossed in a personal conversation. When there was a break in the conversation, she asked where she could get three more copies. Without a word one of them pointed her finger at Ms. Peacock-feather. She said the name of a young assistant who had just left the office. Mrs. Artley went to find her but was told that the assistant had just gone back to the office. Thinking this was like "Musical Chairs", Lori returned to the office to get the three more copies. It seems the young assistant knew nothing about the missing papers and Ms. Peacock-feather finally spoke up saying, "Didn't you know they were just for the new students?"

There was no way of knowing. Mrs. Artley told her there were no directions enclosed, nor where and when to send them in. She also felt they should have listed the names of which students they wanted to fill them out, since they knew who the new students were. Home room teachers didn't but Lori felt that this would be too much for the Registrar's Office to handle. Ms. Peacock-feather then said, "Well, F _ _ k you". Mrs. Artley mirrored her vulgar remark back so that she would hear her words and reflect on her lack of proper vocabulary.

Embarrassed, the young assistant gave Lori the three extras.

Lori left vowing never to return again. Such a run-around, as if teachers had all day to do the work the Registrar should have done. And with no directions.

Ms. Peacock-feather was the same person who urgently requested Lori to letter the word "REGISTRAR" on her door when they repainted it blank. The sign had been painted out and so no one knew where the Registrar's Office was, even though the location was not changed. Seeing the immediacy of the situation, Mrs. Artley stopped in her tracks and with magic marker, painted "REGISTRAR" on the door, and continued on her way.

Even after Lori retired Ms. P. had the gall to call her up at home and ask if she had done any oil paintings of the school. They needed something to give in appreciation to one of the teachers whose work was responsible for getting the school accredited. They wanted to thank her. Feeling Ms. Peacock-Feather's predicament, Lori suggested they give a montage of photos showing all the buildings on campus. Lori asked her neighbor, a professional photographer, to meet her at the school with his camera and showed him around as he took pictures of every area. Then Mrs. Artley rushed the film to the 1-hour development shop, and went to buy a large frame for the pictures. She brought the pictures and the frame to Ms. Peacock-feather, who suggested that the audio-visual department would mount them on the backing board of the frame. They could letter their thanks on the back of the montage and it certainly would be a truly personal token of their esteem for her.

The best part was the school got to keep the negatives for repeat gestures of appreciation anytime they were needed in the future. Sometimes one is really pushing the PUSH door, without knowing it.

(The Computor Stick-up)

In the mid-year on a Friday the students were supposed to receive a report card for the fall term printed by the computer and including their spring schedules. Those who failed a course would automatically be scheduled to repeat the course in the spring. In the midst of this, the electricity went off, as it often did, and one student's schedule was lost in the middle of the machine. The computer would not move when the electricity finally came back on. It was stuck! Chaos reigned!

Special Bulletin

December 11,

TO: All Teachers

FROM: Principal

SUBJECT: Report Cards

Prior to November 7, , we experienced problems with our printer. Subsequently, a smaller printer was loaned to us by a member of this faculty. Recognizing that the smaller printer could not provide the needed service, the school rented a larger printer from a business establishment.

On December 2, , we experienced problems with our scanner.

As of Tuesday, December 10, , I was informed by the company that supplies our equipment that until certain technicalities are resolved they cannot supply us with another scanner.

As an end result I am requesting your cooperation by providing our students with their grades by placing them on the temporary report cards that will be issued by their homeroom teachers on Thursday, December 12

It was too late in the day to call for help. On Monday morning they would have to wait till 11:00 A.M. due to the time difference and phone California to find out what to do. They still had the sophomore and junior classes to run through. This was accomplished by the end of the school day but most of the schedules were incomplete. The computer had only printed LUNCH on the new schedules. When they started the spring term that week, most of the students did not attend classes as they didn't know which ones. The students were loitering all over the school grounds idling the time away. Even the teachers wasted time as they didn't want to start their classes with most of the class absent. They would only have to repeat it day after day until the entire class had arrived.

Finally the students received their schedules but not before the old axiom proved true: "Idle hands make mischief." Vandalism occurred all over campus. To deter this, some of the teachers created various extra-credit projects while others cleaned their cupboards and did things they had postponed for a long time.

All in all, the rescheduling between the fall and spring terms wasted about a month to get the over 2000 students graded, reprogrammed and settled down in their new classes...a month which could have been spent more profitably if they had just continued as they had always done in the past. Without the use of the computer, they had always just continued on with classes til the end of the spring term. Disrupting everything in mid-year with this rescheduling was nonsense!

Enough time was wasted without creating disruption on purpose! When will they ever learn? This was really pushing the "PULL" door on purpose.

DEATH THREATS
(or the school nurses)

Lori's first life threatening experience at Central was when a failing drug-addicted student brought in three seven-foot-tall gang members and told her that if she didn't pass him, they would "do damage". She didn't pass him and damage was done to her car. She reported him in a "Principal's Memo" and heard nothing.

She had her car repaired and got on with her life.

The next was a brain tumor which she attributed to STRESS. It took ten months to find out the cause of her symptoms. Without any neurologist on St. Ursula, nobody knew what was wrong.

When Lori walked she had an imbalance. If she didn't fall, then she couldn't get where she wanted to go. When she was trying to walk left, she went right, and vice verse. Also, when she tilted her head up or down, green lightning streaked around inside her brain, round and round, painfully.

At first she checked with the best ear specialist on the island, thinking it might be an inner-ear imbalance. He prescribed antivert, but within a month she could see that was not it. Then just as he was about to prescribe a Ct-scan, he remembered there was a neurologist now coming from Puerto Rico every other Saturday. Thinking Dr. Dose might need new patients, he told Lori to see her. He was wrong. She didn't need any patients. It took two months to get an appointment and then Lori had to wait until the last one. When she finally did see the doctor, the Ct-scan was prescribed, which should have been months earlier.

By this time she was also throwing up and could not teach anymore. Mr. Treetop, who was sharing his room with her at the time, had to drive her home during lunch period, as she was too sick to even drive her own car. The minute Dr. Dose saw the Ct-scan, she told Bill and Lori to fly over to Puerto Rico immediately. The doctor arranged to have the tumor (the size of a golf ball) removed by an operating neurosurgeon from Spain. Fortunately it was located in a highly operable spot—the lining of the cranium in the back of her head.

When they got to the hospital in Puerto Rico, Lori and Bill had to wait until 11:00 o'clock at night before they could find a bed and then it was the kind with the lower part cut-out, for patients who had to sleep with their knees bent, face down. How uncomfortable! Lori never even knew there was that kind of a bed.

Lori shared a room with a Spanish-speaking older woman. Thankfully her daughter stayed with her and she was bi-lingual. This was a help. Lori's neurosurgeon from Spain could also speak English, but no one else in the hospital, even though English is taught in the schools. The Puerto Ricans would rather that patients should be embarrassed by poor Spanish than themselves embarrassed by poor English.

When Mrs. Artley entered, she was told that the patients were to bring everything such as soap, towels, wash cloths, blankets, basins, drinking cup, pitcher as well as $400.00 to pay the man who would carry the extra blood for the operation. Supposedly the blood itself was free. The nurses said that it was difficult to get matching blood types and sometimes it took two weeks. The place was kept so cold from over-air-conditioning that the patients were freezing, although it was fine for the nurses and the doctors who were moving around. One night when the air-conditioner was going full blast, Lori looked up the word for blanket in her little Spanish Dictionary and urgently told the night nurse she needed one. This nurse seemed to be the only one who was concerned with the welfare of patients and she found one somewhere. Previously, Lori had asked the day nurse and she said there were none. Uncomfortable as she was, Lori was able to get some rest that night with the blanket over her.

The next morning while she stepped into the bathroom someone came in and stole the blanket. She searched the hallways and finally found it in an unmanned dirty linen box marked "CONTAMINATED". Yanking out her blanket, Lori returned to her room and immediately pinned a note to it using her Spanish Dictionary again. It was fortunate she had studied Spanish in high school forty five years ago.

On Monday morning a bright, chirpy young nurse pounced into Lori's room and informed her at 6:00 A.M. that her operation had been moved up. "Jump into the shower and then wait for them to come down and take you up to the operating room right away. They had had a cancellation," she said in Spanish.

Shivering after her shower in that freezing room with frigid tile floors, Lori waited and waited, and got hungrier and hungrier. Hours went by, when finally she made the way out to the nurses' desk. There in broken Spanish, she asked when she was going to have the operation. No one knew but she learned that no one had informed the man who was to bring the back-up blood, so he would be doing that at the regular time, unless he had to spend two weeks finding her blood type. Who knew?

Mrs. Artley then asked to speak to her doctor within the next ten minutes, and when he didn't show up, she went into her room, dressed and went downstairs to the cafeteria where she bought herself a gigantic breakfast. It was the best breakfast she had ever had!

When she returned upstairs, the doctor had arrived. She told him what had occurred and asked him to sign her out. She couldn't recuperate in a Mickey Mouse hospital like that, even though they told her she had only two weeks more to live.

The Artleys returned home to St. Ursula.

The first day home three friends from Central called and told her, in essence, "You got out of Puerto Rico alive. Now go to the states for the operation".

Where to go in the states? No one in her family had ever had a brain tumor before and no one around her knew anything about them, not even the doctors. That same day their middle daughter, Robin, called from the dive shop in which she worked as an instructor. A neurosurgeon had just signed in for a lesson and after that she would bring him up to see the Ct-scan.

When he signed in before his lesson, all the personnel in the dive shop had come around him and said," We'll give you a free scuba diving lesson if you'll give Robin's mom an operation."

Robin brought him up to the house wrapped in a dripping towel. He took one look at Lori's Ct-scan, calmly saying, "I do three or four of these a week". The tumor was just inside the edge of her cerebellum...a very accessible place. Lori got a plane ticket for Friday, so he could look after her when going back. Taking the Connecticut Limousine up to Dawn, their eldest daughter and husband, Chuck's house in Southbury, she stayed with them til Sunday when they brought her to the hospital.

Just one week later than the aborted operation, Dr. Wrap removed the tumor in a warm, efficient hospital with regular beds and patients didn't have to bring all the "extras". Lori had only one more week to live.

Dr. Wrap, that neurosurgeon, had been sent from above. Why had Lori been spared? There must be something more she must do before leaving this world. There must be something more that God had in store for Lori to accomplish in this life.

The growing tumor was squashing the dendrites inside the back of Lori's brain. Dr. Wrap had drilled the golfball-sized-hole UNDER the widest part of Lori's cranium and dropped the tumor down as gravity helped him remove it without its breaking.

Now the overhang of Mrs. Artley's cranium protected the hole which was only covered by her skin and hair. It wasn't necessary to have a metal plate. With the hair covering as it grew over, only her hair dresser knew. It did take some time to gain back her speech, caused by the dendrites being too crushed together to transmit messages to each other. She would leave off the endings of words when speaking or writing, but everything came back in time.

Several years later Lori recalled the incident which must have triggered the whole situation. Rather than the stress endured, she remembered falling backward on New Year's Eve and injuring her cranium in that exact spot from which the brain tumor was removed. She was wearing a long caftan which caught under the heel of her shoe causing her fall. Afterward resting for a short time on the couch, when the pain went away, they all went out for dinner, never thinking about it again. Then she realized that incident was the cause.

About a month after that operation she was back at Central, preparing her students for their midterm exams.

Another year, Mr. Snow, the school maintenance man had to go off-island for a knee operation and asked Mrs. Artley if she would turn on the air-conditioners in the Fine Arts Building for him. She was not a good choice as turning them on curtailed the early morning meetings which she had to attend before coming over to the Fine Arts Building. After school it was hard to remember to turn them off, and several times she had to return to the school after driving home.

The band teachers would have been a more suitable choice as they had before-school rehearsals, as well as after school lessons and they needed to have the air-conditioner on. Finally they took over turning on their own units but Mr. Snow should have given them the rest, while away.

One morning while Mrs. Artley unlocked the door for one of the air-conditioners, she pulled on the light switch and looked up at the thermostat, to fix the temperature as soon as the lights dimmed. Sychronizing the two ascertained that the added wattage of the air-conditioner was putting the surge on the supply to the lights. At that point the temperature should stay put. Although this air-conditioner had been reported from the beginning as a "lemon", the company would not replace it because of the unpaid bill. The school system would not pay until it was replaced. The principal, Mr. Buffalo-soldier, assured Mrs. Artley that it was under warranty for six months, and yet it wasn't replaced until years later and by another company. Consequently, as Lori was looking up at the temperature and the dimming lights she felt a painful sting down on her sandaled foot. Quickly looking down, she saw a streak of gray fur rushing back to his home under a board and a spurt of blood shot up from where the painful sting emanated.

Figure 22

Rat Bite

She put a sign on her room door "NO CLASS TODAY" and limped to the nurse's office. The nurse gave her an ice pack to keep the swelling down and she made her way downstairs to get the form to bring to the hospital. Ms. Grumbles, the only one who could find the forms in her file drawer, was out at the bank. Even though time was of the essence, Lori had to sit down and wait half an hour for her. When Ms. Grumbles came back she had to take a half hour to recuperate from her journey to and from the bank. Finally, Ms Grumbles searched for the form in her files. After all that painful waiting Mrs. Artley filled out the forms and had to, then, get the principal's signature. Since she was too shaky to drive to the hospital, they called Bill to come. Once at the hospital she was supposed to sit for hours waiting until they finally would have time to treat her rat bite. A person could die in that waiting room! Lori was trembling so badly that her husband called the attendant who placed her on a cot in the store room and gave her a shot. Consequently a doctor finally came in and saw the tooth marks. He poured Betadyne over the wound and generously gave her the rest of the bottle to continue at home.

As she was preparing to leave, a woman stumbled into the store room with a bloody cloth held over her forehead which had been cut. She lay down on the cot and a nurse brought her ice in a cloth to hold on it and left. There was no way to hold the ice there so her husband and Lori searched the storeroom to find some bandage to relieve her arm from holding it. When Lori left she had a nauseous feeling about the local hospital and vowed never to go again unless dead.

When Mrs. Artley returned to school the nurse asked if she was "accident prone"!

That school was so UN-safety conscious that it was hard NOT to be accident prone. Among other hazards all over the school, they had placed a large air-conditioner sticking out of a classroom at head height. It protruded out about three feet into the path next to the building. On rainy days, there was no other way in from the parking lot except for that path and a steady stream of students and teachers alike would traverse it as it was on higher, and thus drier land on which to walk. Everyone was looking down to see if their feet were getting wet and thus one after the other would bang heads into the corner of the air-conditioner.

The steady stream of students and faculty alike would make their way to the nurse's post every rainy day with matching bloody gashes in the forehead. When it happened to Lori, as she entered the school infirmary, there was a student with such a large red cut on his forehead that she was sure he'd be scarred for life. One of the male English teachers was also seen that day with an identical bandage. Most of the campus population had identical forehead bandages, in fact.

Figure 23

"THE AIRCONDITIONER PROTRUSION"

After that Mrs. Artley wired on wooden legs to the posterior of the air-conditioner, painting them with red stripes and taped signs on both sides saying: "DANGER" so that people would be alerted. It cut down on the gashes that year.

After Mrs. Artley retired, Mr. Past saw to it that a cement walk-way was laid into the opposite side from the building with the protruding air-conditioner thus correcting a problem that had been going on for years. How many students and faculty had to suffer concussions we'll never know. It was probably being stifled for fear of all the lawsuits in years to come. They were always pushing the "PULL" door at Central.

6

KNOWLEDGE IS POWER

(or the teachers)

In general Mrs. Artley got along with all the teachers. Lori never understood how some teachers had time to play card games with other teachers during their free periods, such as bridge or scrabble or how other teachers had time to lounge around the teacher's room dozing on the couches. One time one of them actually used the teacher's room to sell commercial cosmetics. A male teacher walked up to her folding table and squished a lipstick in the palm of his hand, saying, "Oh, I thought it was plastic." Then he walked away without even paying for his damage.

Nobody thought very much of him after that and Lori was annoyed when they asked her to make a sympathy card for his wife when he drowned later. She did have sympathy for his wife for having married him so she made the card on which all the teachers at Central signed.

The worst teacher she ever came across was Mr. Truck. He even "cut" his own art classes. She couldn't imagine how boring they must have been. He only made lesson plans when forced to by the vice principal, and he rarely taught the students what he wrote. The below-average students liked this because the class was so easy. Once in a while he would borrow a video tape from the Curriculum Center and show "Black Power" or something similar. Nothing to do with art, but the students enjoyed watching.

He was negligent in teaching the students any art because some day they might surpass him. How insecure! Real teachers are proud when they have students who can surpass them.

Mr. Truck came to Central Annex when the tenth graders were put there due to over-crowding. The ninth graders were already kept in the Junior High, so all that were left at Central were the eleventh and twelfth graders. Scandalous tales of what went on at the "annex" ran rampant: about the lack of learning; the teachers taking off whenever; and there was such need for chairpersons that often brand new teachers were given that chore. They hadn't the slightest idea of how to get their department to pull together, like a team. After rooms were rebuilt, the tenth graders were moved back to Central, along with a few of the extraneous teachers.

Central didn't have room for all the extra teachers from the annex, but some like Mr. Truck, had friends in high places. One year he was such a rotten teacher that the head of the Art Department, Mr. Hotshot, arranged for him not to have any classes that fall. Mr. Truck still collected his salary however, and just did "special projects" for the principal, such as decorations for the dances or signs. His trademark was to splash "glitter" all over after extruding spray adhesive on the posters and desks in the art room which he shared with Mrs. Artley.

In the art office, he cut mats for an exhibit using no protection underneath, so that the table was forever scarred with gashes.

When Mr. Truck first came, since he was sharing Lori's room, he dragged in a rusty old set of shelves, with no shelves left in it. It was placed in the corner of the room. When Mr. Buffalo-soldier was making his rounds he spotted the eye sore and accused Mrs. Artley of putting it there. She explained that it belonged to Mr. Truck, as he reneged and said "That's O.K. then". They were "army buddies".

That winter, Mr. Hotshot, arranged to leave school to obtain his Master's Degree and Mr. Truck was supposed to take his classes. Mr. Hotshot did everything in his power NOT to have his classes ruined by Mr. Truck, even to giving the cabinet keys to one of his trusted honor students. He gave his art honor students assignments through the end of the term and promised he would be back to grade them. This meant less work for Mr. Truck, who was satisfied to just sign in and then leave for places unknown. One of his students told Lori that he admired Mr. Truck because he collected two paychecks and only did one job.

When Mr. Hotshot left, Lori was asked to take over as head of the department. Mr. Buffalo-soldier immediately asked her to submit three reports which were already months overdue. Then, Mrs. Artley had to give up two of her classes to Mr. Truck, to make time for the departmental meetings and other duties. One of Lori's classes was disappointed that they couldn't continue with the activities planned, but the other had the "gang of five" in it. They were mutually glad to be rid of each other.

As department head, it was Lori's duty to assign new students to classes. They kept coming back when Mr. Truck didn't show up for class. One girl couldn't find his class for a week after assigned to it. After that Lori started to keep count and found that he cut his own classes 73 times in the less than four months left. He also was no where to be found when final exams came. Another teacher and Lori made finals up for his classes, typed, printed, administered, graded and wrote their grades on the grade sheets so the class was on record. It was very difficult to make up an exam for students who had learned nothing. After they were all finished, Mr. Truck appeared and questioned why this had been done.

When Mrs. Artley sent documentation of his absences to Mr. Buffalo-soldier, it always miraculously disappeared. She kept carbon copies and sent them weekly to Mr. Past. But this was no help in solving the problem. Mr. Past submitted his to the principal also. Finally the Superintendent removed Mr. Truck from Central during the summer and put him in an elementary school where the teacher's aides would take over the class when he took his many absences. The principals there put up with him. He was always willing to do their projects even though he neglected the job he was hired to do...teaching.

Mr. Buffalo-soldier was also removed that summer.

Ms. Angel was the exact opposite of Mr. Truck. She delighted everyone with her ability to "sign" with the deaf students. A heavy-set woman with impeccable color-coordination, chocolate colored skin and a ready smile, she was a paraprofessional and attended classes with the deaf students. When she was not there, the deaf students couldn't learn. No one else could communicate with them so unless they watched what the other students were doing, they were unable to follow the lesson. Copying other students is hardly "art".

Sometimes her expertise was needed in two different classrooms at the same time. When this occurred it was a hardship on everyone. Mrs. Artley wished she could have Ms. Angel in every period as she was such a help. Every classroom has some discipline problems needing an adult presence. Lori felt this was so the rest of the class would not be held back or have "loss" of students along the way. Two teachers are really needed...one to teach collectively and the other individually.

The first day Ms. Angel came, after Mrs. Artley had taken Ms. Lash's art classes in mid-term, there was "standing room only" in that classroom.

Ms. Lash had allowed anyone to come in, whether or not they were registered. There weren't enough seats for the art students, let alone drawing space at the tables. When Lori saw this, she realized all those not in the classes would have to leave. After that she seated the three deaf students NEAR the front of the room facing Ms. Angel. Ms. Angel sat in a chair facing Lori to relay her words. The deaf student's eyes were on Ms. Angel's hands. With this help, Mrs. Artley was able to teach those three students along with the rest of the class. Lori knew the fifteen or more non-art students who were "bumped" didn't appreciate this but it was essential to learning which was a priority in Mrs. Artley's classroom.

A month after hurricane Hugo, all the public school teachers were ORDERED back to their classrooms. Lori had to return even though the school was detrimental to the health of all who entered and her own home was not secured. Also only half of the students remained. The other half had been sent by their parents to relatives. Most of the remaining students seemed depressed by the poor conditions both at school and home. All the lettering work the students had done up until that time was water-logged. Mrs. Artley had to "ditto" up those pages for their booklets WITH lettering on, and then leave space for their illustrations of the "Principles of Design", to complete their booklets. The problem was to find a WORKING ditto machine.

Ms. Angel knew of one in another school and she had connections. After school they went there in Lori's little red, two-seat, standard transmission car with the ditto masters Lori had prepared. Ms. Angel knew all the people in the office and explained Lori's predicament. They allowed them to duplicate the many pages needed with utmost courtesy and understanding. Mrs. Artley's classes were back in business!

After that, since Central was put on double sessions, every afternoon the two went all over the island. Some days they stopped at the off-the-beaten-track free food distribution centers where they retrieved boxes of rations given out to the population. Other days they sought out a furniture "joiner" who could put the many pieces of Lori's mahogany china closet door back in order. It had lain in two inches of water on the floor for two weeks after being torn off by Hugo. Another time they went to a screen repair place and Ms. Angel priced screen doors for an elderly acquaintance who was bothered by flies and mosquitoes. He needed one. After a year, his son, who was a carpenter, finally brought a used one and laid it on the wall inside his living room. It had a big hole in the center of the screen, so Ms. Angel and Mrs. Artley put a patch on, standing one on each side. Then, since his son never did come back to put the door up, Lori brought over Bill's power drill and some hinges and put it up. Never having hung a screen door before, it took some trial and error, especially since the builders of that house had not left room for a screen door. Lori managed to place it on the opposite side from the main door but on the inside as that was the only space it could fit. At least it kept the mosquitoes and flies out.

Their elderly friend lived in a housing development while he still could take care of himself, with a little extra help from Ms. Angel who sometimes brought him good food and other necessities. Another time she enveigled Lori to help get all the props for his ninety-second birthday party. She taped lovely calendar landscapes across his livingroom walls so that he would have something to look at there. He spent his final years in a nursing home where Ms. Angel continued to visit him. She brought cheer into his life, as she also did with her extended family all over the island. She traveled around after school carrying a large basket which she shared with everyone she talked to. No one could count how many lives she touched.

Lori thought she really WAS an angel!

Putting on the china closet door was almost more of a challenge than joining it all together. The hinged part had been broken off by the hurricane and the wood had expanded. Lori measured it carefully and brought it down to the carpentry department at Central. Mr. Kann shored it down himself and it was an exact fit when she put it back on the opposite side from before as the edge was broken. There were a few ripples left in the veneer which the joiner couldn't get out. To camouflage them Lori painted a central rosette of various types of life-size, pearlized sea shells and coral which added to its beauty. Lori and Bill needed its vast storage space.

Another outstanding teacher at Central was Mr. Grill, who taught welding and related arts. When he was asked to help around the school with his students, he always made them plan out the project first and then added some extra gimmick which made it better than the run-of-the-mill job. When asked to make metal bars for the doors of the new Fine Arts Building, he made them in the shape of musical bars with notes playing the school song. The notes were then colored using metal paint and unifying art with the music as well as securing the doors.

After the big hurricane all the Artley's sliding glass doors, windows and skylights were broken. Lori asked Mr. Grill to come to the house and secure them. In order to return to teaching she had to leave it all open because of the shattered glass. Now with these bars on all openings, that could never happen again. Mr. Grill brought a student with him, so he could learn the trade as well as help with the job. They measured all the openings accurately, built the grills with exact measurements and came back putting in the strongest and most artistic grills the Artleys had ever seen. There were sunbursts and curved endings to match the metal railing along the gallery edge. Each one fit exactly and they even put in, gratis, an outdoor motion-sensitive light fixture which was waiting to be installed. Mr. Grill taught his students to do strong, beautiful work.

Figure 24

"THE CEILING SAILS"

In his welding room, Mr. Grill also kept a well-stocked full-size refrigerator and a portable bar-b-que which were put into use at any provocation. Great parties were held any time school was cancelled, with dancing and domino games going on out back. It was a perfect spot as it was on the opposite side of campus from the main office. Mr. Grill boosted the school morale, undoing the damage Ms. Grumbles incurred. Custodians danced with administrators and good times were had by all!

Near this room was the carpentry shop, where Mr. Sampson, the left handed shop teacher, held forth. A great asset to the school, he was selected to hang the ceiling sails in the cafeteria made to cut down on the noise. The S.M.I.L.E. group which had agreed to pay for this labor reneged their payment so he just had to store the sails in his locked closet for infinity. They may still be there, as in the meantime the powers-that-be decided to air-condition the cafeteria instead. Lori wondered how that would cut down on the noise. It <u>might</u> lure more students in. In a study, it was found that only forty students, out of approximately 2500, ate lunch in there.

Mr. Sampson's students built the two strong sets of shelves for the art office from Lori's plywood sheets which placated Mr. Teddybear about the storage. When they had the shelves, order came out of chaos.

Later, a pricey wrecker from a service station placed the three huge boulders to be carved with the school initials at the gate. Mr. Sampson drove by in his pick-up truck and called, "I have all the equipment to have moved those rocks into the positions you wanted". NOW he told them! The rocks had only been sitting there in disarray for the past six months where they were dumped. Why didn't he say that before?

Another outstanding teacher was Ms. Twiggy, the teacher of specially challenged students. She talked Mrs. Artley into co-sponsoring their Creative Crafts group one year. This was to be run like a Junior Achievement company. The plan was to sell the crafts made at the end of the school year. This should cover the cost of the supplies and hopefully make a profit. They didn't count on a lack of the students' investment funds at the start so that she and Lori had to purchase everything themselves. Also, some of the severely handicapped students, which Ms. Twiggy taught, wanted to join. Trying to accommodate them at the beginning, they found that when they cut the strings on the newly tie-dyed tee shirts, the group had to be limited to those who had shown aptitude. The group with which they ended up produced not only the tie-dyed tee-shirts, but batiks, plaster paper weights and sport pins with the signs of the zodiac.

Some supplies were difficult to buy on island so it took time and money to get the bright dyes for the tee-shirts and the sport pin making machine. A professional tie-dye teacher gave them some pointers on making shirts in quantity. To dry them after dipping, Lori put up a rack over the sink, thinking that no one would be dumb enough to walk underneath it when the shirts were dripping. The next day Mr. Truck asked Mrs. Artley to tie-dye the rest of his shirt now that it had some drips on it. She should have known!

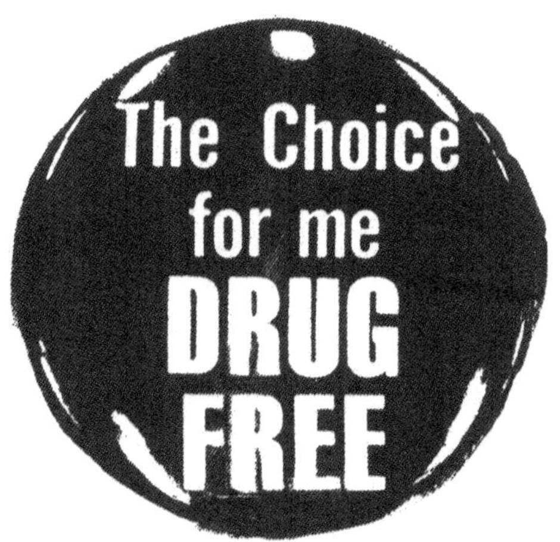

Figure 25

Drug Free Sports Pin

The sports pins consisted of round disks on which they inserted some message and then crimped a celephane outer circle over it with the machine they ordered. Some had pins on the back and on others they placed a round mirror. They were the best selling items, and Mrs. Artley kept them in a large, locked clear plexiglass showcase which she had made.

One day she became disgusted with the whole project. While typing with her back to the door, some student sneaked in and stole the whole showcase. He tip toed out and into the male bathroom where he broke the plexiglass and took out every one of the remaining sports pins. Too cheap to pay the pittance the group was charging, he stooped to stealing something he did not need.

Figure 26

Big Sale Flyer

Figure 27

CREATIVE CRAFTS SALE

After that they would have gone in the red if Dr. Mountain's Drug Free group had not "bailed them out". Some money from the U.S. Government had been allotted for a drug free program so the group ordered 500 of "Drug Free" sport pins to be distributed to the student body. Even though Ms. Twiggy and Mrs. Artley did not receive the money until over six months later, according to the government's usual policy, it finally brought them into the "black". Most of the Junior Achievement companies seem to end up that same way. It is a good first lesson in the business world.

Each school year besides having some club activity for the students, the teachers were expected to join one of the many committees which together ran Central. One year Mrs. Artley joined the Beautification Committee which was supposed to uplift the looks of the campus.

The agricultural students planted two beautiful young traveler's palms which had their long palm fronds in the shape of a fan. They were put at the end of the art building and looked like two proud peacocks with green palms for tails, about three feet tall. That year the grass at the school was being mowed by the trustee-prisoners. After all that work, Lori SAW them mow right over the traveler's palms and be cut even with the grass. In writing, she reported this to Mr. Buffalo-soldier but as usual, nothing was done. After a few weeks, she observed them starting to grow back. She covered them with two aluminum cowls ordinarily used to keep clay from shooting out from potter's wheels. They were like metal bowls with a ten-inch hole in the middle so the roots could still get the sun. When they were about twelve inches high the grass mowers came back and she found the cowls thrown asunder and the small palm trees even with the cut grass once again. Lori was burned," Why try?"

The next year Ms. Sugarmill was the chairperson of that committee, and she tried to plant bougainvillea bushes along the fence and in front of the guard house by the gate. Someone saw them and came in the dark of night to dig them all up. They were all stolen!

That spring Lori had started twenty croton bushes from cuttings at home. When they rooted she potted them in compost. When they had sufficiently grown, she brought them to school and on a Saturday, Ms. Sugarmill, Lori and three other teachers came in to plant them in front of the Fine Arts Building. It took a lot of hard work in the boiling sun but they looked beautiful. The rest of the year Mrs. Artley brought in several gallons of water daily to give them a good start. They were coming along nicely at the end of the school year.

That fall, the Department of Education decided to finish building the upper floor of the Fine Arts Building which had been burned down by the two mischievous students seven years prior. With her own eyes, Lori saw one of the plumbers throw sheets of plywood down from the second floor to flatten and kill ALL of the young crotons they had carefully been nurturing. Such a disregard for anything beautiful made it impossible for any Beautification Committee to function. It was amazing that there was anything left on campus. It was their loss!

Ms. Lash was another remarkable teacher to weather the years at Central. Caucasian, without prejudice, her long curly red hair, trim figure and pretty face made her look half her age.

She wanted to enjoy life to it's fullest which caused her to spread herself too thin at times. Beside being a full-time art teacher, she was taking full care of two rental houses, guiding tourists around the island (among them the Angela Landsbury family), owning a horse and buying her own home.

One morning when she was driving to Central, a truck caused her car to swerve out of his way and roll over, down a hillside, injuring Ms. Lash by slicing her unevenly down her middle. She was taken to the local hospital and it was touch-and-go whether she would live or die. Her classes at Central were put on hold, as substitutes were never hired. Everyday her students would check in with Lori and be disappointed that she was not back. Finally after months she was able to eat soft food, so what did the hospital dietitian give her? Bullion! No nutrition and no calories. Not even chicken soup, but a bullion cube! The island hospital was far below accreditation standards. It had a highly acclaimed building which was shown off in many medical magazines, but inside it was lacking.

Years later when she had finally recuperated, Ms. Lash went to a plastic surgeon, who re-cut her asymmetrical scar. At least it was now in the middle. She was symmetrical again.

At this point she thought she couldn't have children, having no monthly sign and her love life being at its lowest ebb. One of her former students caught her fancy; she succumbed to his charms. The result was an adorable, dimpled mixed-race baby boy nine months later. Though the young father wanted to do the honorable thing, Ms. Lash had once been married and chose to remain just "best of friends" with the father of the baby. His mother baby sat when needed. The growing baby made his mother, father and grandmother proud.

This little love child became the center of Ms. Lash's life; her reason for being. She would have given him the moon if she could. Then came hurricane Hugo and blew away her house ...their clothes, his toys, her furnishings, everything! For a year they lived in the cramped house of some generous friends until she found that due to a series of hurricane loans she could rebuild and refurnish. This took a lot of time, many phone calls (with so few phones working at Central) and much planning.

Like the rest of the island, she rebuilt her home stronger and better than before and it was furnished and landscaped so beautifully that it was featured on the Better Homes Tour that year.

She had a huge bed with a headboard made from 5" diameter bamboo tree trunks and a giant mahogany highboy which enclosed her T.V. and stereo equipment. The whole house and gallery were expertly tiled as well as everything in the modern kitchen. Because of this project, she met and married the tile setter, a Canadian man who had sailed from Trinidad to help rebuild after the hurricane. When the hurricane work subsided he sailed home where he may have had another family. Ms. Lash did not mourn; she had her newly tiled home and her growing boy.

Ms. Lash was undaunted and continued on with her adorable son in her beautiful, new home and teaching at Central, as usual. She often complained of "teacher burn-out". One year she wanted to take a sabbatical leave to write a book, but it was too late when the school finally found a replacement. The wonders of the teaching profession! Ms. Lash never wrote her book.

After school each day several teachers would congregate toward Ms. Lash's room, move all the tables and chairs to one side, sweep the floor, change into aerobic clothes and put a Jane Fonda tape on the tape player. Exercizing on mats, helping one another and joking throughout, they worked out each day after school. At the end, the tape rewound, the furnishings put back, they dressed again. All the rest had wonderful figures while it seemed to Lori that the longer she taught, the more weight she gained.

Probably in any stressful situation, a person eats more than needed to keep up the pace. This continues until the person retires and needs less energy, and less calories. Those who don't gain that extra weight must find their jobs less stressful than their fat counterparts. Lori felt fat and stressed out.

When she first started to teach at Central, Lori heard that Mr. Hotshot would be coming when his replacement was found at the nearby junior high. Lori had been asked to take Ms. Lash's two art classes. She was also teaching Driver Ed which was soon to be dropped due to cost problems. Evidently it took several months to find Mr. Hotshot's replacement as he didn't start his classes at Central until late October.

Tall, dark and handsome with a sparkling smile and very tiny nose, Mr. Hotshot impressed his classes as a strong disciplinarian. His nose had stopped growing when he had broken it at ten years of age. He impressed Lori with his ability to explain even the smallest fundamental details of each art project. When explaining what he expected, he delved into the very depths and there was absolutely no whispering among those listening. Later he relaxed, even to giving certain students the keys to his cabinet. When his air brush generator was eventually stolen, instead of accusing those students, he accused Mrs. Artley, until he found out that hers was stolen also. He learned that thieves had jimmied the door of her locked cabinet to take her air brush generator also. Lori had to buy a truck chain and padlock to secure it after that. Nothing was safe at Central!

When he became the chairperson of the Art Department Lori discovered that he often did not distribute the art supplies when they came in. While the rest had to buy masking tape or rulers for their classes, he had them sitting in his locked cabinet where he, alone, had the use of them.

Since they shared the same room, Lori could not help but hear part of his lessons as she was putting away supplies. She always counted everything and had numbered all material to match the student's numbers. When something was missing, it was obvious who was responsible for its absence. Sometimes she would loan things to Mr. Hotshot, but at the end of the year when asked for them back, he found them missing. He hadn't kept track.

One day as Lori was packing and counting, she couldn't help but overhear him giving his class a lesson in "pissing". He often used the local vernacular so the class would think he was one of them probably. He would launch himself into a soliloquy on certain subjects and "pissing" was the subject on this day. The students scarcely said a word, probably too shocked, and she left as soon as she could.

Some days he would sing songs that he had heard and couldn't get out of his head, like "S...S...Silica". No one joined in. In Mrs. Artley's classes there was a printed rule in the front stating that only those with trained voices could sing in class.

Mr. Hotshot formed the "Fine Arts Honor Class" of art students who wanted to continue on in their art studies and perhaps go to Architectural

College or Art School when they graduated. They were a group of especially talented students and were given more freedom than a regular class.

Sometimes he took them in his Jeep around the island to sketch buildings or landscapes. Other times he gave them outside assignments which they could complete on their own time and hand in by a dead line.

He had them start art college portfolios and took them on a trip to New York City to envision the portfolio exhibit at Pratt each year. They also experienced a New York theater play and other activities which he had wanted to see. He loved to get off the island whenever he could.

Mr. Hotshot learned of the National Art Show sponsored yearly by the United States Government. The winners from each state and protectorate got to have their pictures hung in one of the government buildings in Washington, D.C. for the first year and then sent on a triumphal tour of the states and even other countries. Naturally the winners plus their art teachers were invited to come to the grand opening in Washington which meant a week off for Mr. Hotshot and his protégé.

To get needed things for displaying art at the school, Mr. Hotshot persuaded several of the cutest girls to come with him to the construction companies on the island and "beg" for Upson boards and wood to build display boards. They always got what Mr. Hotshot wanted. He felt teaching them to "beg" was worthwhile.

Mr. Hotshot proposed some worthwhile projects at times, although often he would make his department endure his incomprehensible explanatory mumbo-jumbo first. One time he proposed a "lab fee" like the science department charged. Instead of having to make calendars and greeting cards for the students to sell, they would charge the fee at the start of school and be able to buy all the art supplies never received from the school system. This would enable the ordering of drawing pads for the students wholesale, as well as other necessary items when needed. They could require the students to fill up a certain number of pages with sketches for each marking period for a grade. The teachers would receive some feed back when the skills taught were used. Sketch books would give the students art exercises to do at home and in their free time. Mr. Hotshot cautioned the teachers not to tell the principal as there might be objections. To the art teachers, the fee was a necessity as they had to donate all the lacking art supplies up until now.

Another good idea of his was that the teachers should charge a menial fee for all the art services they were expected to do around the school. Everyone from the monitors, custodians, clerk-typists up to the principal constantly asked for art services "as a favor". Sometimes they even spotted their signs in nearby schools! Signs, posters and murals take up a lot of free time and insinuated that they had nothing better to do. One time the principal asked Lori to letter 300 Honor Certificates over Easter weekend so they could be presented the week after Easter. This would have meant that her whole weekend would have been used up with the project as well as given her writer's cramp. Instead she taught her classes how to letter them, though they had to be presented later on in the year. The students felt honored to have her confidence in them and they learned how to letter in Old English too. That is why art teachers are in the schools—to teach.

There were two excellent projects Mr. Hotshot always had his students do. One was pointelism with which he started off the fall term. It taught perseverance and persistency in order to achieve shading using the black and white medium of the pen point. These drawings were displayed proudly and provided the new art students with a success experience to start off the school year.

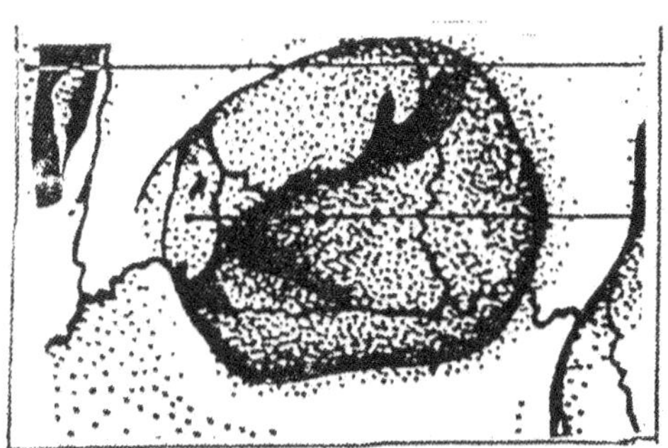

Figure 28

pointelism or stipple

Another project was creating 3-dimensional designs, which showed a cool color scheme when viewed from the left and a warm color scheme from the right. To do this, usually two students worked together, one creating the cool design and the other the warm, with tempera paint on paper. When dry, these were accurately measured and cut into one-inch strips which were alternately glued horizontally on a sheet of oaktag. He liked to use file folders for the oak tag. When all was dry, the oak tag was creased and folded back and forth, like an accordion, they were mounted and proudly displayed and the students marveled that from one direction the viewer received a completely different feeling than from the other.

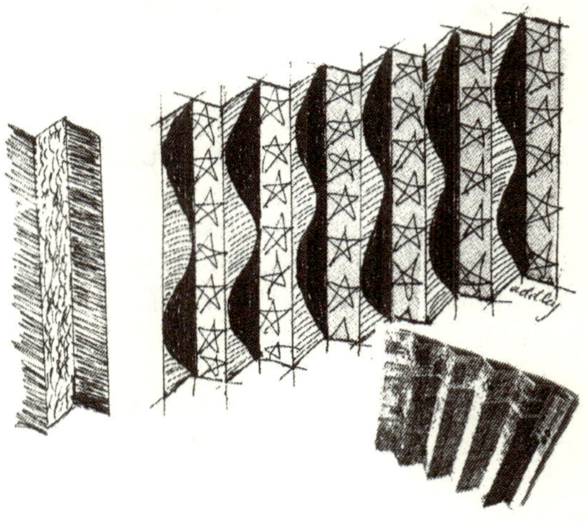

Figure 29

Folding Fan Project

Beside teaching the color schemes, the cool colors (green, blue and violet) and the warm colors (red, orange and yellow), it taught paint mixing with tempera paint, accurate measuring, and cutting with an exacto knife with padding underneath. The students were proud of their finished products and it was impressive in art displays.

The only problem came when the two students who had cooperated, working together, both wanted to take it home. Which one would get to keep it?

Mr. Hotshot became very buddy/buddy with his advanced art students, but after he got married they still came over to his house too often. The Hotshots finally had to move to get away and even had an unlisted phone number. This was changed several times. Mr. Hotshot had to protect his home. He once confided to Mrs. Artley that he couldn't report Mr. Truck's lack of attendance for fear of retaliation on his children. When he left school to work on a Master's Degree, the school straightened out Mr. Truck's problems, without Mr. Hotshot.

When Mr. Hotshot came back from pursuing his degree, he hadn't completed it yet. He couldn't understand how the department had managed without him. Even though most of the teachers had Master's Degrees already, he seemed to have a "superiority complex". He tried to find fault with everything accomplished without his input, as he endeavored to gain back his former position of chairperson. Before Lori retired at the end of that term, the principal required another set of Accreditation Papers to be filled out by each department. They all had rated the school so low on the first set that it would never be accredited. He emphasized that the positive things should be accentuated. The former principal who made Lori send in their accreditation papers plus the two other sets of papers in such a rush, saying they were late, could not recall where he had placed them. The new principal made everyone do it over again, and read them to the other teachers. If the school didn't get accredited, he said it would reflect on them.

Lori was glad to be retired by the time the school became conditionally accredited the following year.

Although the classrooms of course belonged to the school, the teacher who occupied them most of the day referred to that room as "my room". In Mrs. Artley's room she noticed that over time splashes and ink spots occurred on the wall over the sink. Remembering how the tropical mural painted in the Craft's Room had camouflaged the muddy hand prints on the handles, Lori painted a tropical garden on the wall over the sink. It had hibiscus, crotons and a century plant in it and covered all the splashed spots. Mr. Hotshot had been designated to take over that room when she retired. He soon informed Lori, at a department meeting, that he would be using the room around the sink to display pictures. This was ridiculous in a thirty foot room as he had plenty of dry space to display student works. Mrs. Artley explained that the wall around the sink was not suitable for anything of value due to the splashes and ink spots. She could see that he was just asserting himself. He was probably annoyed that there was something in the room that HE or his students had not put there. Three years later, that painted garden still remained there on the wall in back of the sink. He must have realized it had a purpose besides bringing the outside in.

One time when the art department was having its picture taken for the school yearbook, Mr. Hotshot casually announced that the group would meet in the Art Office that afternoon during sixth period. Any with classes that period were supposed to put a sign on the door that there was "NO

CLASS TODAY". He did this without conferring with Mrs. Artley, the chairperson.

Lori went directly to one of the vice principals, Ms. Sorority, and asked her to attend as mediator, as she felt there might be trouble. When they were all assembled, Mr. Hotshot's main bone of contention was that Mrs. Artley was treating the other teachers like children. If she was, it probably was caused by them acting like children...especially Mr. Hotshot. When the principal called for reports, some of them never handed anything in as well as breaking other school rules. During any meeting held, some teachers would play cross word puzzle games showing disdain for the meeting going on.

The music segment immediately excused themselves when they saw what was coming. They always handed in their reports on time and did not play games during meetings. The remaining art teachers said that when they didn't hand in reports, Lori should merely tell the administration that they didn't hand them in rather than to "bug" them for the reports. Mrs. Artley explained that if they just turned in the reports this would be avoided. Their salary included writing up reports about their classes.

Next they did not like Lori to write suggestions in their plan books. If she had anything to say they wanted it to be written on "pastees" which could be removed. On checking with other chairpersons, their suggestions ALWAYS were written directly in the plan books. It was the department chairperson's job to do each month. Just to keep them happy, Lori used pastees for the next two months when school ended for the year. It didn't make that much difference.

Lastly, they didn't know that it is the chairperson's responsibility to look after the department office. They felt annoyed that they could not cook and eat lunch in the office. When there were food sales, they wanted to store the food in the 9' x 12' office, along with the thirteen easels and stacks of colored paper and other art materials. There was no other storage room. Mr. Hotshot wanted to sell popcorn out of the office.

After that meeting Mrs. Artley dittoed signs stating the rules of the office and put three of them up around the room. She kept the ditto master in case those disappeared.

Shortly after this meeting, one of the teachers held a food sale and cooked hot dogs in the Art Office. This brought Mr. Moresum, the head monitor, and Mr. Teddybear, the principal, over to inspect. The smell permeated the air-conditioning vents and announced the project to the whole building. It distracted the students right before lunch. The three signs were still up in the office, stating "Cooking in this office is not allowed." They said Mrs. Artley had done all she could so the disciplining was up to the principal.

Another time was when Mr. Hotshot asked one of the monitors to bring in her popcorn machine. The delicious aroma went through the air conditioning vents again just before lunch period, alerting the ever-hungry students that a Popcorn Sale was imminent. Mrs. Artley was teaching her class at that time when Ms. Sugarmill, the head of the math department, stormed into her room in protest. Together, they went down the hall to the Fine Arts Office to find a monitor and a student in there with many bags of popcorn to sell. The two completely ignored the notices still up in the office but no one had asked for any permission or paid any attention to the signs. Mr. Hotshot was quite annoyed that he had to move the whole operation over to the cafeteria, next door, as he lost valuable sales.

Figure 30

THE ART OFFICE POPCORN SALE

If he had only asked for permission he could have learned that it was against the school rules.

At the end of the term the lock on the Fine Arts Office was changed as forfeiture of its key was the penalty for breaking the rules.

At the end of the school year, Mr. Teddybear asked Lori for recommendations for the future head of the department. She had to tell him that there was no hope for any of them. Mr. Hotshot got the title by default.

MS. QUEENIE

One very kind teacher Mrs. Artley met when she first came to Central was Ms. Queenie. She helped Lori greatly the term she taught English, due to the sudden English teacher shortage and the withdrawal of Driver Education from the curriculum occurring simultaneously. After the pleading of a mother at the PTA meeting, Lori volunteered to teach it even though she was not certified. After all she was certified to teach other subjects and she did speak English.

One of their English projects was to understand Shakespeare's "Julius Caesar" and it was she who gave Lori her two-page outline. Without it, neither she nor the students would have known what was going on in the play. With Ms. Queenie's outline, they all enjoyed the play, acted it out and saw it on the school television, too. They really understood it by then and were sad when they had to finally move on to other English projects.

Outline of JULIUS CAESAR

ACT I

- A. Background
  1. Caesar's triumphant return
  2. Crown offered 3 times to Caesar and refused three times.
- B. Soothsayer's warning
- C. Brutus admits concern over Caesar's rising power
- D. Cassius begins to persuade Brutus to join the conspiracy
- E. Caesar expresses distrust of Cassius
- F. Casca recounts that Antony had offered Caesar the crown three times and that Caesar had refused it three times.
- G. Letters are planted in Brutus' house.

ACT II.

A. Brutus decides to join the conspiracy
B. Decision is made to spare Antony's life
C. Caesar ignores soothsayer's warning and his wife's dream
D. Artemidorus' warning is ignored

ACT III. (The high point of the drama-the rising action ends with the climax, the assassination of Caesar. The action takes place in one day, March 15, the Ides of March.)

A. Caesar ignores soothsayers warning and Artemidorus' petition
B. Caesar refuses Cimber's petition
C. Caesar is assassinated, uttering as he falls, "Et tu, Brute!"
D. Antony's servant secures his master's safety
E. Antony's bold appeal gains Brutus' confidence
F. Cassius is unwilling to let Antony speak in the Forum, but he is overruled by Brutus
G. Brutus wins over the crowd with his speech, justifying the assassination "...not that I loved Caesar less, but that I loved Rome more."
H. Antony gives his speech, reads Caesar's will, and stirs the crowd to rebellion
I. Conspirators flee the angry mob which mistakes Cinna, the poet, for Cinna, the conspirator, tears him to pieces.

ACT IV (One and a half years after Caesar's death, Rome is ruled by a triumvirate—a three man rule, Antony, Octavius and Lepidus.)

A. Quarrel between Brutus and Cassius
B. Brutus decides to march to Philippi
C. Appearance of Caesar's ghost (a forewarning of Brutus' downfall)

ACT V

A. Supernatural omens
B. Antony defeats Cassius
C. Brutus overcomes Octavius
D. Cassius commits suicide. As Cassius dies, he says, "Caesar is now avenged."
E. Brutus commits suicide. (Brutus, having been visited by Caesar's ghost, says as he is dying, "Caesar, now be still."
F. The conspiracy against Caesar is defeated and Antony and Octavius emerge triumphant.
G. The play closes with Antony's tribute to Brutus, "This was the noblest Roman of them all.

The sight of a rat running around her classroom caused Ms. Queenie to jump up on a folding chair, unfortunately falling and breaking her hip. It took so long for her to recuperate that she decided to retire, rather than risk more rats in the classroom. The school missed her, but the rats endured.

She was best friends with Libby Eastend, and the three were chosen to select the furnishings for the four teacher's lounges. Libby was the only teacher in the school who asked all the other teachers to call her by her first name. Lori overheard a young teacher who tried to explain why she couldn't do this because, she said, "Using a title is a sign of respect". So it is that at Central, all those over eighteen are called Dr., Mr., Mrs., Ms. or Miss by their colleagues.

They measured the lounges, drew floor plans, visited furniture stores and wrote up the specifications but what was finally purchased for the school was purely coincidental. When the furniture was put in place, none of them wanted it to be known that they made up the selection committee. All Lori could say was that it was furniture. It didn't fit into the niches and had the cheapest construction possible. Even the fabric was in poor taste. When finally the straps below the cushions broke as Lori knew they would, the pieces were hauled out never to be seen again. In a few years the school needed new furniture again.

This furniture was needed in the lounges, such as it was, but in one of the lounges the cushions were stolen the first week. Lori measured the size and ordered new ones in solid color which coordinated, from a Sears catalog. Then the straps broke, so she bought new ones from a local upholsterer and cut them to size and screwed them into the old nail holes, right in the teachers' lounge. That chair was needed in that place! Then one summer it disappeared. She tracked it down to another lounge where it had been stored. She inveigled one of the prisoners hired to empty the trash barrels, to carry it up to the other lounge while Lori carried the cushions. It was again back where it was needed. That chair persevered until someone again stole the cushions. Then on a weekend, some thieves came in with a pick up truck and carried out the matching couch. After that Lori bought matching locks for the lounges and Mr. Snow put them on. Trying to teach the head custodians how to open combination-type locks was like "extra work" to them. It was obvious if they were to keep furnishings of any caliber, the lounges would have to be locked after school each day.

In light of how thieves would haul anything away, it's a good thing the Administration bought such cheap furniture. There was no sense to try to fix anything up.

They were always pushing the "PULL" door.

There had been a Marine Biology course for seven years which made sense on an island in the Caribbean. Although the teacher had ordered books several times, they never came. Then a newspaper article stated that the island had to hire marine-biologists from off-island because no one had the training for that government job opening.

At a steering committee meeting one of the vice principals commented on this matter saying, "I thought we received those books.", but he didn't know where they were. On further thought he was sure that they came to the school, but no one told Mr. Dapper, the teacher of Marine Biology. No wonder off-islanders had to be hired for those jobs. The Insular-Commissioner of Education was also at that meeting and said the teachers had to "bird dog" those requisitions, pounding and beating everyone who must sign to get them through. They would have no time left for teaching, if they had to do this also. Teachers had done this but had specifically been told NOT to do it anymore. Teachers were not even allowed to go down to warehouse as it would "bother" the people working there. No wonder so few books and supplies came to the school.

Then the teachers were all buzzing about all the NEW books that were being thrown away in the Department of Education dump. After school a bunch of teachers in pick-up trucks went over to the dump. There they found not only enough brand-new Marine Biology books for a whole class but a host of books for other subjects being taught. There were all the books they had been ordering in vain, ready to be ruined by the rain or burned by the caretakers of the dump. Lori wondered, "How did all these books get there?"

Not only did the Marine Biology students benefit from those books but a host of other classes as well. If one person had not heard about this fiasco, all those books would have been destroyed. Perhaps this had happened before and no one knew about it. A book is a terrible thing to waste!

Figure 31

NEW BOOKS IN THE DUMP

Students and faculty alike had a high regard for Mr. Treetop. He was six foot, six and taught ceramics during the day coaching the girl's basket ball team, and later tennis team, after school. Often the school neglected to provide clay for the students so there was no way that the ceramics class could progress and it was very frustrating for its teacher. When they built a second high school, Mr. Treetop moved in hope of finally having better conditions, but for the first year the classroom was even lacking desks for his students. Finally the furniture arrived for his classes, also clay and a large new kiln was provided. At last the class was ready for action by the END of the school year.

Years before he had been the department chairperson at Central, and Ms. Grumbles, the clerk in charge of the purchasing of supplies had a delightful crush on him, unbeknown to Mr. Treetop. Whenever he handed in a requisition for the Art Department, it was promptly filled. They were overwhelmed and wanted him to stay on beyond the three years allotted for each chairperson, but to no avail.

After that a constant supply of art materials was over. When the pencil sharpener in Lori's room broke from over-use, she had to beg for one from the school principal as Ms. Grumbles had told her there weren't any. It happened that there were two of them in a cabinet downstairs in what was called "The Dungeon". It had two inches of water on the floor, so Ms. Grumbles would not go down there. Rather than to fix the leak that caused the two inch lake there, the school plodded along year after year without making use of the conference table, supplies and school records which lay mildewing in the dampness. Mrs. Artley volunteered to get the pencil sharpener as it was needed by her students. Ms. Grumbles unlocked the iron guard doors and told her exactly where it was in the store cabinet. Wearing her usual water-proof sandals, she cautiously waded through the water, retrieved the pencil sharpener and locked up, returning the key to Ms. Grumbles with a "Thank you". Lori missed having Mr. Treetop as the chairperson.

Nothing ventured, nothing gained.

The Fine Arts Department also had a great choral teacher in Mr. Streetheatre. When he first arrived his room was not finished yet, so he practiced in the keyboard room. When his room was finally pronounced ready, it was found to have two leaks. One was from the roof and the other one was from the ground underneath the cement floor. It seems the gutters had never been connected on the roof so all the water fell directly next to the corner where a miniature estuary developed on the floor inside. Mosquitoes were laying their eggs in it, actually hatching out and biting the students during practice. The room also had its own air-conditioner, which kept it so cold that no students could stand sitting in the metal folding chairs. Not to worry! Mr. Streetheatre didn't want his students sitting to sing anyway. The lungs, larynx and diaphragm sound better when the singer is standing.

The real problem was the circulating cement dust from the floor. By the time students left after one period of having their mouths open most of the time, they hardly had any voice left. It was detrimental to the health of their teacher also, as he had to stay there almost all day.

Whenever he could leave his room, Mr. Streetheatre did, to survive. On nice days, he would take his guitar and his classes outside. Sitting under a tree, each group would sing in harmonic parts. Somehow they accomplished the impossible! They performed at thirty different places outside the school that year and even traveled to other islands, staying in the best of hotels in donated rooms. What excellent experiences for the students! What wonderful Public Relations for the school and the community! It broadened horizons and gave the choral students a vocation or a hobby which they would enjoy pursuing the rest of their lives.

There were certain places that Mr. Streetheatre would not allow his chorus to perform; one was the school gymnasium. The school was used to having the chorus perform at graduations as well as for school assemblies, but the acoustics there were impossible. Mrs. Artley told Mr. Streetheatre to just make a tape of their choral selections which could be played over the microphones on cue. This would probably be a truer sound than if he had the chorus stand in the middle of that huge barn-like structure and produce sounds which were less than harmonic.

There was no way to lock the two doors of the choral room because one summer, when students were hired to paint the building, they were not supervised sufficiently and both locks were jimmied. Sometimes students were in there eating their lunch and leaving all their trash or practicing the piano or making love. One time a vandal had come in there and removed most of the ivory keys. Mr. Streetheatre was devastated.

He couldn't bear to even look at the mess. Fortunately the vandal had left the ivories so the next day Lori brought in a jar of contact cement and glued them all right back on. Then she quietly polished the whole piano and seat, which were perpetually covered with cement dust, and left so that when Mr. Streetheatre found it, he might think it never happened at all.

At the end of each year, Mr. Streetheatre always threatened to leave and go into one of the many other professions in which he was certified. Thankfully it was just the end of the year stress which everyone suffered. Lori felt that he was SO good at what he was doing, he never could be replaced.

The two band teachers were also irreplaceable. They were both dedicated but one was older and more experienced. They came in October, the year following Hugo and all the band instruments had blown away or been stolen. Also no students had been signed up for band.

The legislature voted to buy all the instruments new.

The storage closets in their room had no shelves, and one of them had been taken over by the school to store toilet paper. Slowly the instruments came and the students followed.

Unfortunately the counselors had not funneled those new students who had been in the junior high bands into band classes in the high school. In order to have practice it had to be either before or after school. By the time the band teachers, Mr. Horne and Mr. Leadfoot, had gotten the students screened and organized so they could practice together, it was the end of the first term. Lori wondered, "How were they ever going to get a band together by the end of the year who could play the graduation march?" Somehow they accomplished this monumental obstacle. It, was amazing considering all the mountains they had to climb that year.

The next year was better. The school had received eighteen piano keyboards with head phones and had a classroom reserved for them. When a student played the keyboard, s/he could hear what was played through the head phones. The only problem was that there was no teacher. Mr. Leadfoot had been one of Lori's former Driver Ed students in her first class at Central. Now he was all grown up and a music teacher.

That summer, she phoned him at home and found he was off-island, so asked his mother if he could teach that class. She said that he had taken piano lessons so he undoubtedly could do it, especially to beginners. Much to his consternation upon his return, he became their new keyboard teacher.

Figure 32

He always finishes first

Due to the room shortage, Ms. Dzienis' science class was also slated to use the keyboard room when there was no class there. Soon the head phones were disappearing. They were down to only twelve, and the science class was getting the blame, even though those students would probably not have any interest in them. When Mrs. Artley saw this situation developing, she canvassed the whole campus for a room for the science class. Nobody would share a room with them. They had all kinds of reasons. Finally, in desperation, she turned to the cafeteria. There was no chalk board there, and the dietitian said they would have to move the chairs and tables away from the rest, and then move them back at the end of each day. She was the only one who had room for the science class and at last, they were out of the key board room, which was completely unsuitable for their needs. Ms. Dzienis was gratified that her class was out, but extremely disappointed in the science chairperson who should have taken the initiative in finding her a room.

At the end of the school year, Mr. Leadfoot adamantly refused to teach that keyboard class again. To avoid further problems, Mr. Teddybear, who had taught that class before becoming principal, agreed to teach keyboard for the following year, if Mr., Leadfoot would take over for him when he had to attend meetings. Mrs. Artley wasn't there to find out how this worked, but she hoped they got replacements for the six head phones that had disappeared.

The other band teacher, Mr. Horne, with previous band experience in the states, understood how to attack the various problems which arose from time to time. He started a half-year "History of Music" class alternating the following term with "Music Theory". The problem was that there were no books on either subject.

Due to the great book mix-up which emanated from the inability of the Department of Education's Office of Procurement to read its own invoices, fifteen books which had undoubtedly been ordered by the local university were delivered to the Coordinator of Music and Art in the public schools. He glanced at one book and said they were history books, mainly because they combined music and art with history. He gave the box of books to the Coordinator of History and Social Studies, Mr. Black. Mr. Black glanced at the books, and realized they really were music and art books. Since he knew Mrs. Artley from an organization in which they were both active, Phi Delta Kappa, he carried them over to her room at Central. Lori happily accepted them and then after seeing them, Mr. Horne declared they were exactly what he needed for his new courses.

They gave a comprehensive history of musical instruments from the dawn of time to the present, illustrated. Neither knew that there was such a book coordinating world history with the arts. The books were kept and well used. "But what about the university teacher who had ordered them and never knew what happened?", Lori wondered.

The band continued to grow and progress. It went to Washington D.C. for the inaugural parade and performed all over the island. The Jazz Ensemble was seen everywhere on the island that anything was happening and was in great demand. Their Spring and Christmas concerts were enjoyed by all who attended. They had an active booster group which raised money to make it possible for them to accept an invitation to Denmark. Lori thought, "No one would know today about their humble beginnings after the big hurricane."

They pushed the "PUSH" door that time!

One year when Student Council Elections were coming up, Ms, Sheboygan, a young native English teacher went to the Audio-Visual Aids Department and asked that a sound system would be positioned outside the main office for the nominees to announce their platforms to the crowd which would gather. Unfortunately, Mr. Lumpenprole, the director, was out at the time so she left the message with a student. By the time Mr. Lumpenprole received the message, he realized he couldn't do it but never communicated this to Ms. Sheboygan. The candidates were assembled the next day but the listeners couldn't hear them. They had to deliver their speeches at the top of their lungs to those few who were within ear reach. This lack of communication was the cause of basic problems all over Central.

The following day was supposed to be Student Council Election Day. NO ballots were placed in any homeroom mailboxes for teachers to distribute; NO ballots were delivered to homerooms during homeroom period; NO voting was done that day. Due to this, election time was extended to the next day. Finally by the end of the week the ballots were counted, but the new officers could not be revealed till the following Monday. This was typical and ran rampant along with the consequential last minute changes in planning everyone had to endure year after year in every field.

Another example of this lack of communication was the Identification Photo Caper. At the beginning of the term, each student paid three dollars as s/he had a picture taken during school time for Identification Tags which would be delivered at some future unknown date. Meanwhile none of the some 2500 students could ever be identified. Nothing was heard about this until months had elapsed.

In November the Daily Bulletin announced that I.D. Tags would be distributed that SAME day. In order to do this, the powers that be expected the entire tenth grade to cue up outside the main office. This was a little over one-third of the school population.

The Junior class was to line up outside the cafeteria and the Senior class was to squeeze itself inside the library, which in no way could accommodate them. This could not be explained to the students as Homeroom was held _after_ they were told to be in their lines. They had to hear about it through the grapevine. By the time they got the system going, it took up the whole morning.

Many times other students would come into Lori's room to read the bulletin as their Homeroom teacher never came. But there was no way of notifying students of happenings such as this which occurred BEFORE homeroom unless it could be read by the students a day or two BEFORE it happened.

Giving up that morning of teaching meant that all their morning classes were one more lesson behind the afternoon classes. If the teachers had only been informed of this half-day of not teaching, they could have brought in reference materials to review or books to read. As it was, it also wasted the teacher's time.

The administration always flaunted its motto "Education is our priority", but Lori could see that by not planning ahead or communicating in a timely manner, they made a joke of that slogan.

They were continually pushing the "PULL" door.

Figure 33

"Photos this way"

Specializing in combining world history with that of Africa Mr. Dine, made the subject come alive for his African-American students to whom his teaching was most meaningful. Often he was chosen as head of the Black History Month Conference held each year.

At the end of the term in June, he asked Mrs. Artley if she would paint portraits for him of the great African Kings and Queens from the past. This would have taken up all summer vacation and she still wouldn't have gotten all of them. How did he know that Lori had a complete set in full color which her husband had given her years ago from the Budweiser collection? They were all laminated and ready to hang in his room, and she had no further need of them. Long ago she had xeroxed them so that they would be in tints and shades of gray for her art classes. They were inspiring models for her students when working in conté crayon. By eliminating the full color, they could focus on the highlights and shadows easily, which was the real purpose behind this lesson.

Therefore, at the end of the summer, Lori was glad to present the set to Mr. Dine to use for decorations in his room. They would aid greatly in his teaching as well as fill the room with color. He was overwhelmed and told her that this was the best gift he had ever received in his life. He put them up around the room with temporary adhesive strips.

The following year, Mr. Dine died and all the pictures "disappeared". No one knew where they went but Lori was glad she had given them to him while he still was alive and teaching. She knew he appreciated having them. Maybe he took them with him!

SCHOOL SCANDALS

Although Mrs. Artley didn't have time to listen to all the scuttle-butt between teachers and students there were a few stories going around that other teachers insisted on telling her.

One was when Ms. Southern Belle went to court on a school day because she was being sued by her plumber. She told the judge she hadn't paid him because when he was finished she promised to "give him a little something". The man clearly wanted just his money in payment, not a "little something".

The judge slammed down the gavel, commanding, "Pay the man".

Figure 34

SCHOOL SCANDALS

Another scandal was whispered to Lori in confidence by a colleague who confided that Mr. Buffalo-soldier had propositioned her a few years prior. He invited her to go to Puerto Rico with him for the weekend. Not being into dating married men, she replied in the negative, and ever since he had been taking it out on her. He really did play some dirty tricks on her which could have no other explanation. Since the conversation between them had no witnesses, there was no way to prove "sexual harassment".

The campus was agog when the parent of one of the female students punched Dr. Freeman in the nose in front of his science class. At the time, Lori didn't know him, but after the big hurricane, the transom was open between their rooms, and she and her class could hear him, first hand, propositioning his young female students. Many times Lori's students, who were also listening, unavoidably, wanted to go in there and clobber him. Mrs. Artley had to calm them down and get them back to work.

One day, probably to maintain discipline, Dr. Freeman put the class down by saying, "You are the children of slaves. I have always been a free man, therefore you should listen to what I tell you." His class work was so poorly organized and he mixed propositioning his students with the lessons so it was a blessing when he finally retired and went back to Africa. Science teachers have always been hard to get.

Another sad case was that of Mr. Squash, a young math teacher who was selling high grades in his class for money or sex. Math was required for graduation so some students may have fallen into his trap. The "good" students did not have to put up with that so he was removed abruptly in the middle of a term. When Lori ran the Job Bank, she recalled some of the students who had worked for him requested NEVER to be placed with him again. They wouldn't tell exactly why.

A school is no place for that kind of extortion.

Then there was the tale of the parent who found a note from a male teacher in the trunk of the car his daughter had borrowed the night before to go to the library. It said, "Please don't wear panties tonight". The teacher was dismissed summarily and the daughter was transferred to a private school.

There seemed to be no stigma to girls coming to school in maternity dresses and even unmarried teachers did it. Sometimes the students even held baby showers for them IN SCHOOL. The girls were allowed to attend classes until the seventh month and resume three months after the baby was born. It seemed that half the girls had babies at home, which they would bring to school to show off and be admired by their classmates, teachers and the young student-fathers of the babies.

In some schools, students who parent children must continue in the Adult Education Division and obtain a GED diploma. In some cases, only the young mother is punished, but Lori felt that the young fathers are equally to blame. They bring another child into the world whom they can't support. "They should attend classes to teach them about parenting and supporting the child to the age of eighteen", it seemed to Lori. "The course should also include birth control."

In one of Mrs. Artley's classes she overheard the following conversation between two female members:

Obviously pregnant girl: "Wouldn't you want to show your love to your boyfriend by having his baby?"

Other girl: "No, I would NOT want to have a baby now. I have plans to go to college and have a career. If I was dumb enough to get pregnant, I'd have an abortion".

At the end of that period, Lori took her aside and said, "Right on".

Several of the male teachers who were still teaching had impregnated students, but the girl's single parents did not wish to "rock the boat". They did not report it, probably not being sure of WHO the father of the child was.

One of the female teachers, Ms. Lamb, reportedly had a child by an administrator. His wife told him that she would divorce him if he paid one cent toward child support. The child was growing up without a father.

Lori was sure there were others in the same category.

Often unqualified women were placed in no-work jobs at school because they were the concubines of those in policy making positions. Usually they couldn't do the work because they had no training so they goofed off as much as they could get away with. They would eat at their desks and make personal phone calls all day. They never had to fear that they could lose their jobs as they were political plums.

At Central, the registrar was accused of raising the grades of certain students or adding courses they never took so that they would graduate. This was sometimes done to insure scholarships for some students but it wasn't fair to the students who earned their grades and worked at all their courses.

Another teacher, Ms. Shoofly, always wore a big wig. One time a photographer asked her to take her "hat" off for the picture. Her handsome husband also taught at Central and one of his students developed a "crush" on him. One day during a confrontation, that girl reached out and pulled the wig off Ms. Shoofly in retaliation. There was nothing wrong with Ms. Shoofly's hair underneath except that it was messily pinned down. Ms. Shoofly just wanted to save time in combing it.

When at long last the district was building another high school, it was rumored that the new Principal and the prospective band teacher (before it was open) were having many secret meetings in the band room.

Even though it opened the following school year, they were short of almost all equipment. That first year Lori wondered how much teaching could be going on.

Next to the entrance of the main office at Central was the main teacher's lounge furnished with love seats, lounge chairs, soda machines and the teacher's mail boxes. There was also a locked closet where once were stored the musical instruments for the band. After HUGO, the closet had been looted and musical instruments marked "CHS" were later seen walking down the streets with their new owners. Consequently, Central had no instruments for a new band until the legislature finally passed an act to replace them a year later.

Figure 35

THE ORANGE PAPER INCIDENT

After the hurricane, the windows of the teacher's lounge needed replacing. About ten huge sheets of clear Plexiglas were put in exposing the teachers in the lounge like a goldfish bowl. To effect an immediate cure, one of the teachers asked Mrs. Artley to paint landscapes on the Plexiglas to create some privacy. In the interest of expediency Lori spent the evening doing a small example to show the principal, using acrylic paint. The next day Mr. Buffalo-soldier took one look and promptly vetoed the whole idea in his own inimitable style. His long range plan was to have the huge windows covered with silver mylar, which would act like a mirror on the outside but create privacy on the inside. This could not be achieved until the following fall term, however. The teachers steeled themselves to becoming "goldfish".

The principal never liked any ideas he didn't think up himself.

One morning Lori came in and found that some of the teachers had covered all the windows with rolls of three foot wide orange paper. They must have done this in desperation and it probably did create privacy, in its own shocking way, the night before. The following morning it had all fallen off onto the floor. The masking tape they secured it with could not handle that tremendous weight and they had wasted the whole roll.

Probably the perpetrators were too embarrassed to clean up the mess and the custodians said, "That's not me job, mon". Considering the weight she might lose bending down and picking up all that paper, Lori cleaned up all that mess. At least some of the paper was recyclable and she stored it in the Art Office, in rolls.

In the fall term Mr. Buffalo-soldier came through with the mylar, and the windows were covered, but not before students outside had seen many eye-brow-raising scenes inside the "goldfish bowl".

7

CHALK ONE UP

(or the students)

"Look at all the neck wrinkles!", a front row student shouted out, breaking the train of thought of the entire class. Mrs. Artley was showing how to draw a tilted head for the portraits they were about to start. Lori learned," A teacher should never use herself to show how something is drawn".

For that rude remark which broke the class's concentration, penalties raced through her mind. Should she have Antonio wait until after class? Should she write out a principal's memo and let him handle it? Should she expect an apology? Should she launch into a tirade on his motives? Should she tell him to come around when he's 65 years old and let her count the wrinkles on his neck, if he's still alive?

With comments like this, Lori was sure he wouldn't be alive. Someone would kill him before his time.

Students are much the same wherever they attend school. In all Mrs. Artley's years of teaching in New York State, Ohio, Connecticut and the Caribbean islands, she had noticed their similarities. One of the differences in the Virgin Islands is that the students spoke in their dialect at home and to their friends, but in school they were taught to speak in Standard English. Their dialect was a mixture of their original African accent mixed with the Irish dialect of their ancient overseers. Knowing that, one could understand whatever they said, but the reason they had to learn Standard English was so that they would be able to communicate with an employer some day. This made sense to the students and they cooperated in the classroom.

Teachers notice from year to year the repetitions that occur, and the accomplishment of being able to reach students which comes with years of experience. Lori posted among the other Rules of the Class: "Standard English only will be spoken in this classroom".

Figure 36

THE ARTS CLASS

The first students of whom a teacher becomes aware are the "bad" students, whether it's because of their poor behavior or their lack of learning skills. Secondly one becomes aware of the very good students because they are such a help in class. The middle-of-the-road students are the last to be recognized, but they are the largest part of every class.

Lori knew that sometimes having one good student in a class would stabilize the whole group so that it accomplishes more. The teacher can play to that one-person audience, and the rest of the class listens. Once Lori had the "gang of five" in one class and this undermined all learning activities. Most of the time was spent disciplining them...wasting the time of the rest of the class.

Among the bumpy road of teaching, Lori had met many students who enriched her life as much as they did the classrooms. Sometimes this was hilarious and sometimes tear jerking. At times she heard about experiences from other teachers but all impacted her life and the lives of their fellow students.

The very first student who impressed Lori was a talented young man in the fifth grade in the Endicott, N.Y. school system. One project they did was textile design where he brought in a plain white table cloth from home and proceeded to stencil his original designs neatly around the edge, making it a cloth of great value. This was the way he tackled all the art projects, with great interest and a long attention span. It was no wonder that he would pursue the field of art when he reached the point of attending college. It meant some research on his part to find Mrs. Artley's Philadelphia address by then, but he wrote to her there, asking recommendations for colleges offering the best art courses.

Visits from former art students always pleased Lori, as they do most teachers. It reminded her of her mother's experience long ago. When a language student in a Manhattan, N.Y. high school researched her address years later (the numbers of the streets had even been changed). He still found her in Queens. He appeared at her door one afternoon to say "thank you" for passing him in high school so that he could then attend college in the fall. In those days one could only enter once a year, and if he missed that Fall date he probably would have followed another path in life and never attained his dream of becoming a doctor. She remembered the incident so long ago when she gave him the benefit of the doubt so that he got a passing grade in German. For this he was eternally grateful to Lori's mother and it weighed on his mind some twenty years. Her mother didn't win her Phi Delta Kappa key for nothing!

At the opposite end of the scale, a very strict history teacher at Central, Ms. Cruikshank, suffered from painful burns when someone put an unknown substance on her desk chair. She thought it was glue when she felt the liquid, but it turned out to be some kind of acid. She was out for the rest of the school year. Since there were no substitutes and history was compulsory for graduation, her students were the real losers. They had to pay to go to summer school that year.

Then there was "Hitman", one of Mrs. Artley's art students. He explained that he had gotten that nickname because he "hit" on girls, but from what Lori could see, it was guys, too. In class he always did his best to follow all instructions to the point that he became a very fair artist by the end of the term.

The following school year he joined Ms. Lash's Painting and Drawing class. He brazenly told her that he didn't have to learn anything. "I just do what Mrs. Artley told me last year." Lori was glad she had time to cover watercolor painting at the end of that year, as some years there hadn't been time.

Later, he got into an argument with another student as to who was the best art teacher at the school. He said that Mrs. Artley was and got into fisticuffs with the other student. They had to be broken apart. Later Lori told him that no one is the best in everything, but all teachers had areas of expertise.

After he graduated the Artleys encountered him at a classy restaurant on the island. He was all spruced up, in full dress, bright eyed and bushy tailed. He was the head waiter. No longer the "hitman", he was now "in control" and on the road to success.

One Friday at Central, shots rang out. A student had carried a gun to school and there was to be a "gang war". The gangs were affiliated with the junior high schools from which the students came. Now attending Central, Lori felt they should have become unified, but they still knew who came from which school, despite the banning of identifying caps, jackets or jewelry.

Near the spot where the "rumble" was to occur sat Lori's student, Hercules, talking to a friend. In the midst of their conversation they heard the shots and their instant reaction was to run in the opposite direction. That was the wrong thing to do as Mr. Moresum collared them as they crossed paths, thinking that they were involved in the fight and getting away. He dragged them to the main office where they were accused of running from the scene of the crime. Lori felt what they should have done was just found a near place behind a trash barrel and sink down to the ground unseen.

In the principal's office, Mr. Buffalo-soldier believed Mr. Moresum of course, and put both students on suspension right at the crucial time of missing their final exams. They were also given the "work duty" of moving about 100 boxes out of the cafeteria. Two monitors stood over them like Simon Legrees to see that the task was accomplished to the last letter.

Mrs. Artley wrote a letter on behalf of her student, but it was ignored in lieu of Mr. Moresum's testimony.

Later the real culprits were caught and expelled, but it was too late. These two had already failed their exams even though innocent. Such is the course of "blind justice".

Another one of Mrs. Artley's students was Webb who attended both her Basic Art and Graphic Arts classes. One day he came huffing into their room saying he was just talking to two friends when the boyfriend of one suddenly came up and punched the other one in the nose. A fight ensued and he was just about to get into it when a monitor appeared on the scene. Webb quickly changed his mind and ran to class to explain why he was late.

Facetiously Lori asked him who was more handsome, the girl's boyfriend or Webb's friend? He thought for a moment, shrugged his shoulders and said "How should I know?". He was only looking at the girl.

Webb was always falling in love that spring. He made everyone aware of his attraction to another member of the art class, Adlyn, when he penciled pictures all over her portfolio. When she discovered his advances she immediately erased them.

After class, he followed her out of the room but wouldn't let her leave the building for her next class. She called to Mrs. Artley from her place of imprisonment. Lori came and escorted her out the door. Lori knew she crushed Webb's ego when asking him to leave Adlyn alone. He didn't get it even though Adlyn repelled his advances every step of the way. He continually maneuvered his desk to be close to her and she continually changed her seat to a desk as far from him as possible. At the end of class Mrs. Artley would tell him that she was not returning his advances. He retorted, "But she really likes it".

It was very hard to teach the principles of design when their teenage minds were on L.O.V.E.

In one of Webb's classes there was Easy Squeezy, a girl who thought she could get through art on her looks. She had a good figure and boasted to the class about having "had" all the boys in the back of the room. Webb was always looking for a girlfriend and asked Lori whether he should choose her. In all candor, Mrs. Artley replied," Not unless you want to get AIDS." He didn't.

Easy Squeezy was very vociferous about the clothes Lori wore. She kept commenting on Mrs. Artley's crocheted blouse worn with a color coordinated pair of slacks. Easy's comments that it was "form fitting" caused Lori to slump all through the art lesson and never to wear that outfit to school again.

To put an end to this waste of time, Mrs. Artley made up a little speech which she used on subsequent occasions: "The only reason we are all within these four walls together is for YOU to learn about art...so let's not waste anymore of our valuable time on what you are wearing or what I am wearing. Spend as much time as possible on ART, the purpose for which we all are here."

Due to certain student's commentary about clothes, Lori avoided wearing not only the crocheted blouse that coordinated with those woven slacks, but any knitted slacks, too. Woven fabrics were usually O.K. A delightful kaleidescope blouse was avoided as it reminded one student of a rug she had, and any animal print clothing turned certain students "on". Otherwise, Lori's wardrobe sufficed.

One day, Helvique, an extraordinary, quiet young lady of dark beauty, aspiring to be a model, came into the art room at lunch time even though she was not in any art class. The regular art students came to work on their art work, enjoying the air conditioning and the soft music that played from the radio.

Suddenly, breaking the silence, a LOUD, shrieking S-C-R-E-A-M filled the air! It broke the serene ambience they all enjoyed. They all looked at Helvique who explained she was reacting to something she saw. She never would tell what it was.

When shortly after that she decided to leave the room for a short time, one of the regulars, Roscoe, picked up all the belongings she left and was ready to put them outside the locked door when she came back. He told her to stand back, and then threw everything she had left out into the hall. Trying to close the door again, she was quicker than he, and plunged her foot inside.

Usually Mrs. Artley tried to stay out of the student's petty conflicts, but she saw this incident. Lori was on the other side of the room when Helvique came back inside. Helvique's good breeding made her come over and apologise to Mrs. Artley and the class. She had figured out why they had thrown her things out.

Lori told her she would have to learn to control her reactions and her voice if she planned to be a model. This appealed to her sense of propriety. Their ear drums were spared the rest of the year.

It was Mrs. Artley's habit to chalk a line on the board whenever she won a point during a class. It gave added emphasis as well as brought out the few times she had won in a world where the students usually did. Sometimes she chalked up three or four lines during a day.

One day when she was focusing on the techniques for drawing eye expressions, Aloyishus, one of the more brazen students, asked, "How do the eyes look when a person is having intercourse?" Mrs. Artley replied, without batting an eye, " The next time you're having intercourse, call me up and I'll come and draw your eyes".

The class roared and Lori chalked one up for herself on the board.

Another day she heard another student, Enio, remark to his neighbor, "You're a dummy!" To that, Mrs. Artley could not help but reply, "Everyone is a dummy sometimes". Enio retorted, "Not me. I never do dumb things." "That's the dumbest statement you have ever made", Lori retorted.

The whole class roared in approval, and called out "Chalk one up for yourself!" which she did.

Cartooning was the lesson of the day, so Mrs. Artley drew a three picture cartoon on the board about this incident, to show them the process. Each segment became a picture; the words were lettered in guidelines so the captions were in legible Gothic capitals; and she showed the class that cartoons such as this occurred every day. They just had to recognize them and put them into pictures.

"It would be tempting to stop teaching and just draw the many scenes around school that were humorous. Everyone would get a few laughs!", Mrs. Artley felt.

The class said to chalk another one up.

Bully Dickens was a female student and worse than any male Mrs. Artley had ever met. Bully was in one of the two classes Lori had, to free Ms. Lash for the chairperson position. When Mrs. Artley took over that class, orientation was long over and well into the second month of school. Bully decided that she would help by taking attendance each day, as Mrs. Artley didn't know the student's names yet.

She also marked students present if she had seen them in school that day, whether they came to art class or not.

Another thing her unsolicited help rendered to the class was repeating Mrs. Artley's directions for class projects as if they shouldn't do the project unless the words came from Bully's mouth. Mrs. Artley could see this was going to lead to problems as Bully didn't do any work herself. She went around the room shooting the breeze and supposedly helping all the other students. Biding her time, Mrs. Artley put up with it until finally Bully was absent for two weeks, due to illness. In that time, Lori oriented the class to her rules which were posted in front of the room, and took the attendance each day herself, noticing that many students who were marked present brought absence excuse notes from home.

Figure 37

"The Dummy"

Then Bully came back.

Explaining the current assignment to her, Mrs. Artley asked her to get right to work so that she would catch up. She was non-plussed and resented the fact that she could no longer play teacher. A few days later she got into a "knock-down-and-drag-out" battle with Lori and if it weren't for Lori's aerobic work outs, Bully would have happily caused Mrs. Artley bodily damage, throwing her onto the concrete floor. Lori stood her ground. She told Bully to leave the room and go to her counselor, while Lori wrote up the incident on a principal's memo. On its reception, vice principal Ms. Sorority called her mother in for a conference.

The whole episode was reiterated as well as another incident Bully had tried to instigate. Bully had told her work table, "Now watch this". As if to sharpen her pencil, she made her way to the desk, and then when Mrs. Artley's back was turned to lean over a desk to help some students with their drawings, Bully used her freshly sharpened pencil to try and undo the stitches in the back of Lori's slacks. Mrs. Artley swung around and though Bully tried to side step, she was the only one out of her seat. She incriminated herself.

When these occurrences were presented, her mother tried to turn the blame on Lori, instead of realizing that her "innocent little angel" could ever do such things. Ms. Sorority said her older sister was the same way when she was at Central. Their mother always turned a "blind eye" to their capers.

Mrs. Artley refused to have her back in class as she was so disruptive. Her former teacher, Ms. Lash graciously fitted her into one of her three remaining classes and saved the day. Bully's schedule had to be rearranged but Lori was happy never to have to see her again.

Central finally graduated Bully just to get rid of her.

In Lori's second art class, there was Maximillian, a six foot tall young man with everything going for him except an inferiority complex in art. Since he thought he could never do any assigned art project, rather than even try, he handed in the teacher's sample taped to the board, putting his name on it. He knew so little that he thought it wouldn't be recognized. When confronted, he would lie a blue streak insisting that it was truly his work. It was almost as though he really believed he had done it.

Finally Mrs. Artley had to write up a principal's memo about him, as he never improved though he was caught each time. Ms. Sorority called his mother in along with Maximillian and Lori. Ms. Sorority always arranged the office so there was no seat for the student in question. He had to stand, weak kneed and weeping through the entire time.

His mother started off berating him for wearing his one gold earring. "You didn't have that thing in your ear when you left the house this morning!", she shouted as if he were hard of hearing. "Take it off right now!"

With that constant badgering that eighteen year old young man was broken down into a crying child, calling her "mommy", and pleading to her to believe his lies. She knew him better of course and we all realized that if he got away with it now, he would continue the habit of lying throughout his life. He was then in his senior year.

They decided that his only punishment would be to redo the art work: an architect's rendering of his dream house, which he would hand in with his own name. After school, he and Mrs. Artley started to do this. He asked, "How do I begin?"

Mrs. Artley had gone all over this, step by step, with the class already. Where had he been? Lori had to teach him in baby steps how to do each process, and finally when he got to the painting part, he ruined it, and had to give up. Although he had claimed that architect's watercolor painting he had handed in was his own, he still didn't know how to do it. They could both see the difference in the two watercolor renderings-his and the first one he handed in. There was no way to rescue his work, so they decided to leave it there and go on to the present project on which the class was now working. He looked relieved. Everyone can't be "good" at all types of artwork and Maximillian had learned his lesson.

Each project assigned used a different medium and utilized different skills. If a student couldn't master one skill or medium s/he might find encouragement in the next project. Before the end of the term, most students found several art skills and media which they could master.

Lori hoped that Maximillian will find one someday.

In the class that Bully had left, Lori had room for one more student now. She was replaced by Lori's all-time pride and joy: L'overture, a short, handsome young native originating from Haiti.

He had asked her three times, but she always said there was no room for him. The chaos in the room was too much to even think of adding anymore students. He hadn't pre-registered for any art classes but he needed one more class to graduate. Mrs. Artley's goal was to gain control of that class, but she admired his persistence in tracking her down all over campus, so she finally took him in conditionally. They agreed that if he gave her any trouble in that class, he would leave voluntarily.

He was a total joy from the first day he came. When she was giving directions, HE listened. Others, watching him, realized there was a connection between listening and knowing how to tackle problems. The whole class improved.

In every test he earned 100%. He studied. Since there were four sitting at each table, Mrs. Artley dittoed up four different tests on the same subjects. This cut down on the copying. The same questions were used, but on one test they formed matching questions; another had them as True and False; the third test would have them as fill in the blanks; and the fourth would have them in the form of multiple choice. Also included were simple art cross word puzzles, time lines, compositions and pictures to be drawn. It was more work for Mrs. Artley, but it was the only way to find out what the students had learned. L'overture's presence raised the class average.

The following year they chanced to meet while crossing the campus in opposite directions. He told Lori that he missed her class and having art. Mrs. Artley missed having him as a student also, but at least her classes were better that year. Being able to orient them at the start made all the difference.

After he had graduated and grown to manhood, he came back to the school to visit. When Lori knew him he was the same height she was. Now he was over six feet tall. He told her that someday he would build that dream house he had drawn. It put her into a reverie as she remembered those difficult days at the beginning. Lori hoped she would be there to visit that wonderful "dream house" someday.

In the Craft Room where the students worked with clay, the doors to the back cabinets were always full of student finger prints. With the opening and shutting of the cabinet doors all day, there seemed to be no way to keep the room looking decent. When they were cleaned off, the next class would put the finger prints back on. They would have to be camouflaged in some way.

To do this Mrs. Artley developed a tropical mural in the same proportions as the row of cabinet doors. Utilizing all types of tropical vegetation, ocean in the distance with islands, parrots and egrets flying across the foliage would do the trick. After school on Friday afternoon, she sketched the scene with a marker. Then on Saturday morning, Prince, a talented Afro-American student and she started filling in the spaces using the acrylic paints in her box. She selected the color for each item and he filled in with long graceful strokes in the shape of the foliage. The final combination of tropical colors looked very Caribbean and remained there years after she retired. It really camouflaged the finger prints and set the theme for the room. The doors never needed scrubbing again, whether pulled or pushed.

Prince went on to Art School in the states.

BAD ATTITUDES

Sometimes these bad school situations created poor student attitudes, while other times erratic home lives caused dysfunction in school. Lori could see that everyone suffered when this occurred.

A cartoon in the local paper showed a student with a Mohawk haircut and mask holding a gun. The caption was "When a semi-automatic pistol was found on a 15-year-old girl, the CHS principal put minds at ease, saying, "The gun was not fired and wasn't pointed at anyone. There was no fight."

That was in their local paper, but a nationally syndicated cartoon about that same time showed the whole country or maybe the world that school problems were universal. Lori saw in the first picture two professors walking along together, talking: "The world is crumbling". The next picture states, "Students were asked to take the responsibility for their own performances, but now, if a student fails, it's our fault." The third picture said," Bringing home the report card is not as we knew it." Exit the two professors. The last frame showed a father and child with her report card. The father spoke," I'm very disappointed in your teacher." "Me too, Dad" replied the daughter.

One such experience Mrs. Artley had was when packing up art supplies at the end of the period. Mr. Hotshot was starting his lesson with the following class. As she left, he handed her a piece of paper saying, "Morris, one of my students drew this picture of you". She looked at it. It was her in the NUDE. Then he boldly asked, "Does it look like you?" "No, not in the least", she replied as she walked out.

When her blushing stopped she resolved to have plastic surgery as soon as school finished that June.

THE THEFTS

One night Lori's classroom was invaded and her locked art cabinet kicked open. It was never able to be locked again. Mrs. Artley bought a truck chain, U-bolted it around the middle of the cabinet and padlocked it each afternoon when she left. The thieves had gotten through the outside doors and the double doors to her room, probably using a credit card on the latch.

They had stolen her air brush generator, missing the classes' air brush probably due to the "organized clutter" of the cabinet. After work, she drove to a locksmith shop and bought a steel plate which was bolted across the seam between the two doors by Mr. Snow. A credit card could no longer slip between the two doors to press in the latch. That night thievery stopped, but they grew bolder during the day.

Intimidating the members of the class, five young giants invaded Mrs. Artley's classroom, under the pretense of wanting to borrow something. They didn't know what. The boldest of the robbers came up to Lori's cabinet and reached in, grabbing a roll of masking tape. They had interrupted the lesson sufficiently, so they left. Mrs. Artley was no match for those long legged juvenile delinquents. She decided to prepare for the next visit they made to her room with a pistol-topped plastic bottle full of red batik dye.

Outside the building, Mr. Horne, who recognized them from band class, caught them gloating over their "take". He ushered them into the main office and later told Lori that their real motive was to interrupt the class.

Any students who came in with the same intentions after that found that the red dye marked them well. The monitors could easily pick them out of the crowd.

Some days when the air-conditioner was broken, Lori would open the double doors, since the windows were sealed. She bought a couple of oscillating floor fans which at least kept the air moving and made the circulating warm air more bearable. Passing students must have thought they were opening the doors to put on a show, as they lingered at the doorway, watching the art students work and perhaps, "casing the joint". Having them there made the art students feel self conscious. It was their artwork which should be exhibited. Why should they have to be on exhibition, too?

While Lori was typing one day, alone in the room with back to the door and the radio playing, some student tip-toed in and took the Plexiglas display case with all the sport pins they had made in it. If he wanted those sport pins so much, why didn't he join the Creative Crafts group who made them? After that theft, Mrs. Artley carefully carried the broken Plexiglas case to have it finger printed. She wrote up the theft and put it in Ms. Sorority's mailbox, also, but she never had gotten any response from anyone. Finally she just bought another piece of Plexiglas and glued it in, so it was the same as it had been when she first made it. Since it was so valuable in showing off 3-dimensional works, Lori left it with the art room, when she retired.

It is hoped that students will see the error of their ways as they grow to maturity.

One day an unknown student came to Mrs. Artley's open door and stood there belligerently, watching the class work. Sauntering over, Lori told him she had to close the door because of the air conditioning. Without a word he turned his back and kicked the door shut as hard and fast as he could—catching her two middle fingers of her right hand still in the opening. Blood was oozing out of the crushed fingers, but no bones were broken. Mrs. Artley had to cancel classes and go straight to her doctor because of the swelling and pain.

Since she had vowed never to go to the E.R. room at the hospital since her five hour wait after the rat bite, she received the papers at the office to go to her own doctor who would attend to her needs immediately.

Figure 38

The Kick

Five years later, Workman's Compensation had still not paid him nor had the student been caught.

In one of her classes, Mrs. Artley had a very nicely mannered, tall young man with medium brown skin named Rambo. He did his work each day without comment however she noticed that whenever he was absent, he never brought in an excuse note from home.

She let it go for a while as he always got his work in on time and seemed to do his very best. One day she casually asked him for his excuse note. He told her that he lived in a little house by himself and there was no one to write it. His older sister lived on the other side of the island and he couldn't get over there to get a note before school when he had been ill. He was such a nice addition to the class that she just let it go, no matter how many absences he had. Natives from the other islands often sent their children to the U.S. Virgin Islands as education was free.

Another strong and talented student in that class was Santillio who told Mrs. Artley that he had defended his girlfriend from a man with a knife. He lived near her and admired her from afar. Finally she broke up with the young man who had fathered her child, and after the encounter, Santillio became her new fiancé.

After he had learned Old English lettering in Art Class, he volunteered to letter the certificates for his shop class. He brought them all to Mrs. Artley during her free period, and indicated that he wanted her to help him finish them. He also wanted to use the supplies his class had used. He was such a personable student that Lori's heart went out to him and came through with the lettering. He made a good impression on his shop teacher.

Late in the year, a student wanted to come into the art room during lunch period with his friend who was taking art. He was probably lured by the air-conditioning and the musical ambience. Mrs. Artley responded that he could stay only if he did art work, as his friend was. She gave him some paper to use, but he probably became frustrated at his results, comparing with his friend. He said he wanted to leave but come back. Mrs. Artley said he should either do one or the other, but not coming and going all period.

With that he grabbed his book bag and as he strutted out he called, "I don't want to stay in this "s _ _t h _ _e art room anyway."

"He seemed to have a very limited vocabulary as well as being unschooled in drawing," thought Lori.

When the Fine Arts Building was rebuilt years after being burned down completely, Mrs. Artley was elated to be given the first room, but the air-conditioning made the students catch colds. Lori had to wear a wool sweater to be able to stand the room for the whole day. During the final exams, students shivered and shook with cold for the hour and a half that they had to sit still. In that warm climate many did not even own jackets, although those who did, wore them.

Finally, half-way through the year, one of the brighter students, Galileo, studied the air-conditioning outlets in the ceiling. He noticed that hidden in the corner of each was a small knob. He prophesied that if these were closed, it would cut down on the amount of cold air that came into the room. He and Mrs. Artley went around the room closing all the knobs. He was right!

Afterward, Gallileo asked Mrs. Artley if he didn't deserve an "A" for discovering the knobs. "You should get a zero for not discovering them <u>months</u> ago," she retorted. But secretly she gave him two "A"s.

A scruffy young man, obviously over the legal age to be in public school, was in one of Mrs. Artley's classes. Usually Danny minded his "P's and Q's" in order to graduate, but finally she had had enough. She had to send in a principal's memo because he kept touching girl's "buns" and putting his hands around their necks in pretense of strangling them. This did not only keep them from doing artwork, but he had wasted half of his period also.

Mr. Past, the vice principal in charge called his parents. When parents were called in, it not only wasted their time so they lost a day's pay at work, but they came anytime they wanted without any notice. These came when Mrs. Artley was taking her second period class to see a film on art colleges in the library. Though she would rather have listened to the Admissions Director's talk and see the film, she only had time to take attendance and leave for the parental conference.

Mr. Past, the two parents, Mrs. Artley, Danny and the two girls were at the parental conference. The girls made "light" of the incident, even though in class, they had cried for help. Mrs. Artley had done everything to get Danny to stop, including taking points off his grade, but he just laughed. When she started writing the Principal's Memo, he stopped. Now he wanted his points back.

His step-father told him in no uncertain terms, "Just go to your classes, get right to work and NO FOOLING AROUND—IN ANY CLASS." His step-son had obviously been in trouble before.

The next day in class, Mrs. Artley made Danny verbally apologize to the two girls, the class and herself. She had no more trouble with him. At the end of the term, Mrs. Artley asked Danny what college he planned to attend. He retorted, "I won't say 'cause you might write and tell them not to accept me." They both smiled.

She wouldn't have written nor recommended him either. She hoped that college would straighten him out so he would not be eternally doomed to pushing the "PULL" door.

8

FOR ART'S SAKE

(or articulating with other subjects)

To strengthen teaching, Lori felt it became more meaningful to the students if one subject was synchronized and coordinated with another. This was called "articulating". For instance, teaching not only the subjects being taught at school, but articulating with life in general.

This is teaching the "whole" child and means each subject must not only overlap with other subjects the student is taking but also coordinate with the other courses being taught in the "feeder" schools. In this way, students feel that what they are learning is relevant in today's world and important to living. If possible the high schools should "clue" the lower grades as to what they were teaching so that the students would be better prepared when they moved up. Teachers found a broader scope of what they could teach and students gained insights by combining and building on their learning experiences.

At Central, try as they might, the art teachers never had any opportunity to articulate with the lower level. They did start a group to which the progressive art and music teachers belonged, but since the majority did not show any interest, the articulation of grade levels couldn't effectively be passed on.

The best they could do was hold the meetings at Central so the lower grade teachers who attended could at least see the final projects when high school student works were displayed. Often they would spot art materials in the high school art rooms and beg for items. This left a shortage of materials for the high school students. Meager as the art supplies were, the high school received more art supplies than the lower grades ever hoped for.

ARTICULATING WITH PSYCHOLOGY AND BEHAVIORISM

Finally Mr. Burn-out, the Fine Arts Supervisor, retired and a new and still idealistic former teacher, Mr. Frustration, took over. He tried to hold a one-day conference for all the art teachers and asked certain teachers to present various programs which would help everyone move toward the same goals. They prepared their best lessons, which the others could redirect to whichever grade levels they were teaching. Unfortunately, Mr. Buffalo-soldier, the new principal, felt threatened because he had not thought of this first, so he cancelled it the very day of the conference. All of the students had been given outside assignments in lieu of the missed art class, so they did not come to class that day. Lori spent the day doing reorganization of her art room but felt deprived of this chance to articulate her program with the art programs of the other schools.

The subject of Lori's talk was how to create various moods in a painting. Knowledge of how to create a mood in a picture helps students to speak through artwork, expressing their feelings. Also, they would be able to understand expression in the paintings they would see throughout their lives. Although she used visual arts of different moods with her own classes, she had many work sheets prepared for the conference attendees which went unused. Mr. Frustration never tried to accomplish anything in his new position again. The school system had triumphed once more! It crushed another individual.

Mood identification would articulate with psychology and understanding human behavior. Lori always covered it in her classes but didn't know if any others did.

ARTICULATING WITH SIGN MAKING

No matter what field the graduates went into, there would always be some time in their lives when they would be called upon to make some sort of a sign or poster.

Although Mrs. Artley debated whether to include lettering in her curriculum, she knew there was a great need for this field even though some of the students grumbled. Every job needs signs made from time to time, and if the lettering was poor, the signs would be illegible. This defeats their purpose.

Mrs. Artley was surprised that some students didn't seem to know that space must be left between rows of letters, or that guidelines for the lettering should be erased rather than outlined with black. They didn't know there should be a space between each word, and that the lines of words are easier to read if they are straight on the sign, rather than at angles.

One student told Lori that the only reason he elected to take art was that he heard that she taught four different alphabets in lettering: Gothic, Roman, Calligraphy and Old English. He wanted to learn Old English, so he cooperated all year long until they finally came to the Old English portion of the course. Once he learned that alphabet, he asked if he could continue that lettering until the end of the term. His honesty so impressed her that she allowed him to follow his dream. He made an ambitious collection of poetry in Old English letters. Some of it was unforgettable.

ARTICULATING WITH MATH

After Hugo, Mrs. Artley was privileged to share a room with Ms. Sugarmill, the chairperson of the math department. When Ms. Sugarmill had a class, Mrs. Artley would work at her desk, and Ms. Sugarmill did the same when Lori had a class. Lori was impressed by the wonderful course Ms. Sugarmill was teaching called Practical Math. She felt this course should be required for graduation as it prepared students for all kinds of real-life situations, all needing some type of math reasoning to solve. The students had work books which they took home each night and the next day in class, Ms. Sugarmill quizzed them orally in class. By their answers, she could tell who had done the homework. She kept track of this on 3"x5" cards which she used to calculate their grades. Those who never knew the correct answers were put in a separate pile and their grades reflected their negligence. Whether or not they did homework, her students learned how to solve practically every type of problem they could possibly meet for the rest of their lives.

Another way the Art classes articulated with Math was through a project the students loved called "Line Design". Geometric circles, ovals, rectangles, squares, triangles and trapezoids could be made using the straight lines sewn on 5" x 7" index cards.

First the students would complete an exercize on a work sheet so they learned the concept of making curves by using straight lines. When they handed that in they received a 5" x 7" card, They put a line of equidistant dots on the lined side of the card, vertically and horizontally and numbered from one to ten. Single threading a needle with some bright color Mrs. Artley showed them how to make a large, embroidery knot at the end and start with the first dot. They sewed to the farthest dot and then back to the second dot and so on. Finally a curve would form. Their expertise would shine when the more adept students would be able to

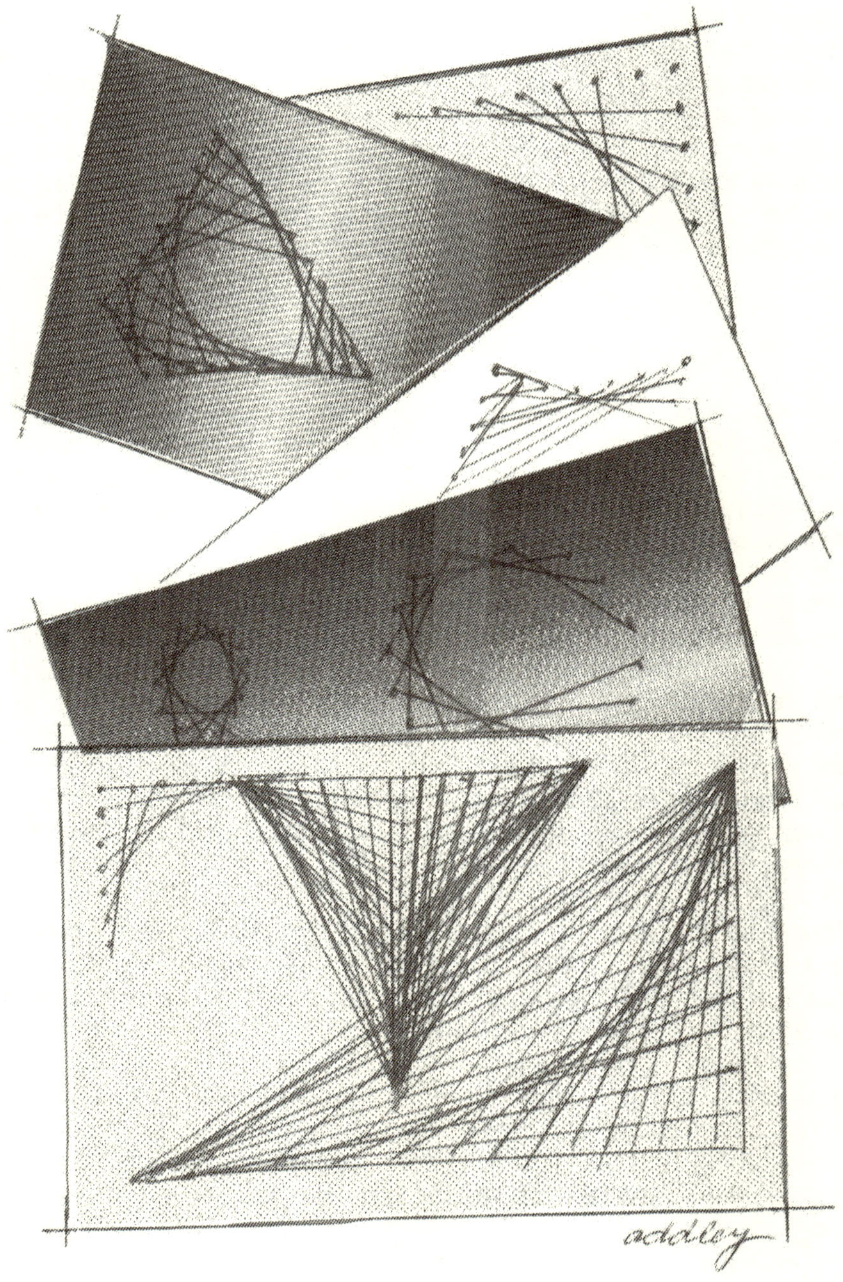

Figure 39

LINE DESIGNS

save thread by making the long stitches on the back of the card with dashes instead. When they were handed in, Lori wanted to see the backs in order to grade them, after which the cards would be mounted on a harmonizing color and the students would letter their names below the picture to be displayed. Some math teachers gave extra credit when the students brought these colorful cards in to adorn the math room walls. Each one was different and there seemed no limit to the number of geometric shapes they could interlock.

The concept of sewing was new to many of the students as well as making a curve out of straight lines. They learned how to end a thread by sewing twice over the threads in the back. Students were very proud of their works and couldn't believe they did such a sophisticated piece of art, articulating with math.

Measuring the distances between dots on the back, or by measuring mats on which to mount pictures also articulated with Math in the Art class. It was necessary to know one thing in order to do another.

ARTICULATING WITH SCIENCE

When they studied the scientific theory of how all colors come from the sun, students would bring up their science books to show Mrs. Artley the very same diagram there. They would nod their heads affirmatively when Lori explained the theory to the art class. Students who had not taken science yet were astounded, but they caught on when Lori showed them how to draw it for the cover of their COLOR booklets. When the sunlight comes down and touches various objects on earth, they asked how come some things are brown or black in color. That brought color mixing in and the color wheel, which took up the pages in the booklet. Lori brought in a prism to show the proof of this theory, and they all had seen a rainbow. She explained, "each raindrop becomes a tiny prism in the sky. That is how we see the rainbow colors in the sky when the sunlight goes through the raindrops. The colors in both instances are always in the same order as on a prism. Scientists have even given each color a number at the place that the color always shows up."

They used the colors for color mixing exercises, and to learn color schemes, which were used in interior design. They would use this knowledge when they had to decorate their apartments or houses later in life. They also used different types of paints which articulated with chemistry, such as what ingredient made acrylic paint different from tempera or watercolor.

In another way, science and art were combined when a pamphlet told of logwood ink made from the heartwood of a tree which grew on Caribbean islands. Down in the rain forest Lori retrieved some logwood limbs which she brought to class. One student took a branch home, shaved it, boiled it and mixed in the alkalie from a used battery. It became black transparent ink, and gave the art class a lifetime supply.

It was one more way chemistry interconnected with the art program.

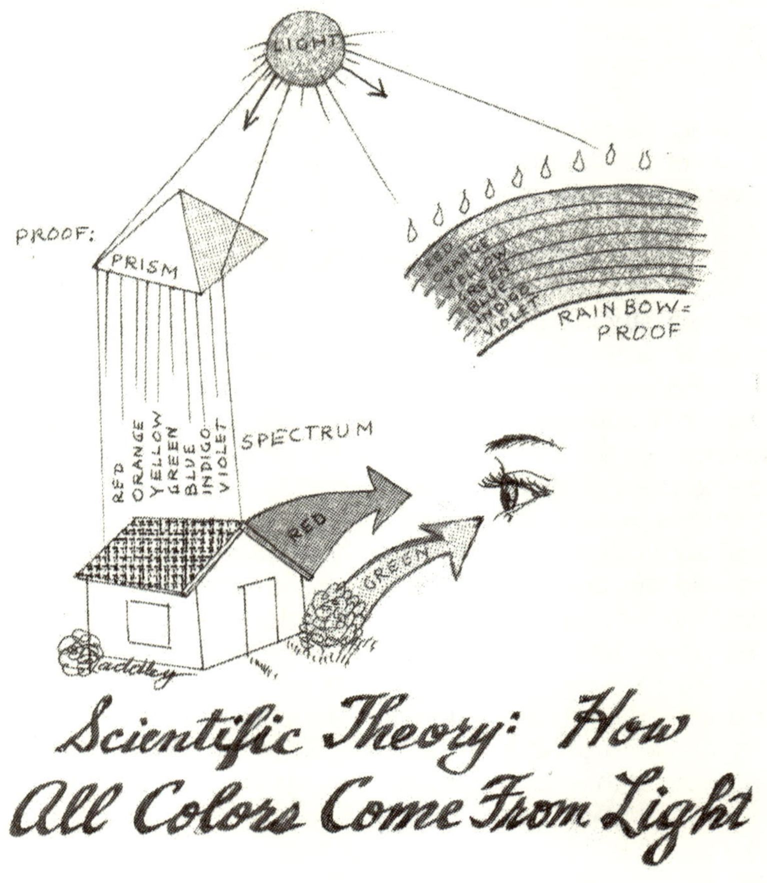

Figure 40

Scientific Theory

ARTICULATING WITH BOTANY

When Lori's art classes were asked to make small signs for each plant at the Botanical Gardens the students learned that all plants had names. The Gardens supplied the small dark wood rectangles and paid for the white, condensed Gothic press-type. The students learned how to measure guidelines precisely and how to center the long words forward and backward with press type. They also learned that each plant had not only a local name but a long Latin name and species, and they learned to be precise. All of this was a new experience to most students. Articulating is learning by connecting.

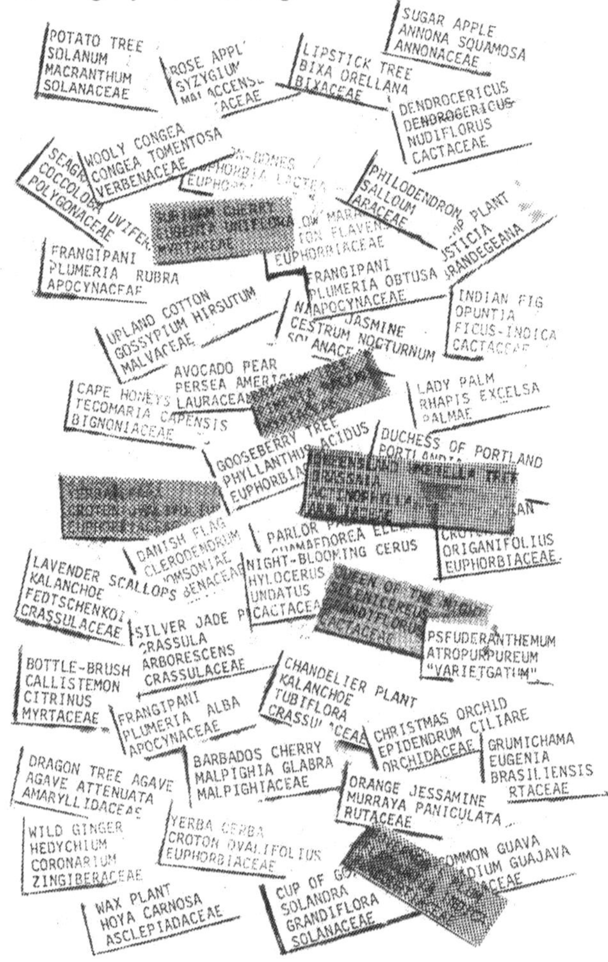

Figure 41

BOTANICAL SIGNS

ARTICULATING WITH ENGLISH

On all art exams an English composition was required. One of the most interesting essays Lori required was when they had just finished studying the sculptural works of Richard Hunt, who started as an Afro-American teenager by welding old automobile parts which he collected at the junk yard. Lori asked the students to describe how they could become millionaires like Richard Hunt by using something people threw away. The answers were very creative, even to how to create solar heating using an old bucket someone had thrown away.

They also articulated with English when they backed up the journalism students with drawings for their creative stories or ads for potential advertisers in the school newspaper.

ARTICULATING WITH MUSIC

Although Mrs. Artley had to keep students from singing in class unless they had trained voices, she constantly played soft music as a background for drawing. She also had a short speech she read to the students about color meaning, made into a rap song by J.J.'s brother.

The whole class participated in chanting it in rhythm using one student, who had been elected leader. This was a more enjoyable way to learn the information and the students wanted to keep the rhythmic words. By the time the test came along, they all knew it by heart:

<u>The Rap Song</u>

COLOR

Color is not something you can be
Color is something you can SEE!

Colors are everywhere...cars, homes and fashions,
Affecting the animal, vegetable and human reactions!

RED is a color, which does it's own thing
Paint the hornet's nest opening, and keep 'em from entering.

That's not all the red color can do-
It makes the whole swarm move elsewhere...just because of you!

Colors also affect the animals called Mink,
Blue cages make them hostile; but docile in PINK!

Tropical fish thrive under a pink light;
80% female makes a good sight...

But under a white fluorescent light, they don't swing,
With that white light, they have 50% male off-spring.

For people, "cool" colors "calmness" commands,
Thus, ocean front property is more in demand!

But reds, violets magenta and pink—
"Warm" colors: we react against—out of sync!

But used in Senior Centers and convalescent homes
The patients will move around with many less groans.

Here, too, use PATTERNS on walls, fabrics and floors,
Patients have time, there, as they have fewer chores.

In drug rehab centers and offices where we wait...
Blues and greens lower blood pressure, and make waiting great!

And paint babies' ceiling with a calming light blue,
Cover all room decorations with cool colors, too.

For the same time colic begins, babies start to see-
If the colors they see are "hot", so will their reaction be!

60% of people prefer blues and greens; 40% are perverse...
Except for Cal., Ariz., New Mex. and Tex. Where percents reverse!

The reason: these people MIGRATED to those states
To FIND the "warmth of sun colors" in their fates.

When you use a color, show what you want others to see...
For they'll interpret colors the way they think—ought to be.

ARTICULATING WITH SOCIAL STUDIES

Their construction of the twenty-six foot long Black History mural hanging in the main office, the creation of time lines put the Old and the New Masters in the proper perspective and the drawings of portraits of famous Afro-Americans from the past were all methods of bringing history into the art curriculum. There was a need to have Black History all year round.

ARTICULATING WITH HOME ECONOMICS

When the art students studied interior design in the unit on COLOR, they articulated each year with Home Economics.

One year a flyer meant for the Home Economics Department was mistakenly put into Mrs. Artley's mail box. Not realizing it must have been a mistake, she read it to her Art classes. The Salvation Army was holding a Dress-A-Bear Contest. They would supply the bears to be dressed and after judging them at Thanksgiving, they would be given to needy children at Christmas.

A number of students signed up for them, happy to take them home but sorry when they had to be returned for the judging. There were two left over, so Mrs. Artley took those home and made girl's clothes for one and boy's for the other, complete with a miniature Virgin Island flag for the boy bear and a parasol for the girl bear... all made out of an old dress she had in her sewing bag.

Lori was surprised to hear on the phone that her bears had won the trophy. It turned out to be a beautiful gold-tone winged lady mounted on a mahogany base. She felt like the only one in the whole world who had a trophy engraved with "DRESS A BEAR."

The following year Mrs. Artley was asked to be one of the judges.

ARTICULATING WITH ARCHITECTURE

When the students drew the floor plan of their "Dream House", designed by themselves, they were encompassing architecture in the art class. They used architectural templates for the furnishings...things they didn't even know existed.

One student drew his home without any bathrooms. "A house doesn't need any", he said. His classmates pointed out that when he wanted to sell his house, no one would buy it. He could understand their logic and voluntarily fitted in two bathrooms.

Some students drew the louvered windows upside down so that all the rain would find its way inside the house. The classes also learned that cement blocks, shingles or bricks had to be placed alternately, for strength. They also learned how to represent various building textures and the floor plan symbols for lights, telephones, and doorbells. The project culminated with a three-quarter view of a perspective painting of the house, like the watercolor renderings done by architects.

Articulating art with architecture caused many students to consider the field as a final vocation as well as plant the idea of a "dream house" in their minds.

ARTICULATING WITH NATURE

One year while wandering aimlessly all over campus due to the continuous room shortage, Lori's art classes realized they were without any room. After sketching trees, rocks and roots for the first month, they were finally given a dirty, dark unpainted room with no furniture in it except a wonderful small sink with cold running water. They were finally in business!

They were grateful to the Vocational Department who had consolidated its classes in order to vacate that room for them. It was the only one available with the necessary running water which was mandated by law for art classes.

Meanwhile, they articulated with nature.

Figure 42
"My Dream House"

ARTICULATING WITH MODERN DANCE

In that bare room, the first thing they worked on were large bed sheets on the floor which the class turned into backdrops for the modern dance class.

First the cement floor was swept and a large bed sheet was carefully laid flat. Certain students showed great aptitude for the project and the rest stood around and learned from them. When the mural was drawn, everyone joined in for the final painting. The modern dance group was very pleased with the outcome.

As the backdrops were being completed, Mrs. Artley searched the campus for chairs each day. The students in other classes would move the chairs outside to sit on during their free periods. They usually neglected to move them back, and these were the chairs that had Mrs. Artley's eye. Behind the burned out building, a few of the desks which had been saved from the fire were stacked. They all were missing a leg or two, but the students carried them back and two were used together to make one table. Sometimes student desks supported a table top at which they could seat four students.

Even though the students did not receive the standard Basic Art course that year, at the final tally, they accomplished more projects than normally. The Modern Dance group used those backdrops for many years.

ARTICULATING WITH POLUTION CONTROL

The advanced art class filled some great needs at the school. One time they cut individual stencils which said "KEEP CHS CLEAN" and went around campus stenciling the message on the outside of every building. The signs constantly reminded students to curb the pollution on the school grounds.

The Landmarks Association called Mrs. Artley one day. They had a donation of 100 heavy plastic blue barrels which had been used to carry hazardous liquids. The only thing they could now be used for was trash barrels with holes drilled in the bottoms. These would be chained to posts next to each bus shanty all over the island. They could be emptied weekly using just one key which would fit all the locks. The main problem on this island was to teach the youths to throw their trash INTO the barrel. The natives had the annoying habit of tossing everything they didn't want, into the bush. This tradition was passed on from generation to generation. When the grass was cut, every so often, all the trash was exposed.

The head of their committee asked Lori if she could have her students paint designs on the sides of the barrels to develop student awareness. The Landmarks Association would pay for all the art supplies they would need, if Mrs. Artley would just make a list. Meanwhile Lori had to find a place for them to work. Lori wished that this came later in the school year when she could have taught the students the Principles of Design but the Landmarks Association wanted them done immediately.

Figure 43

THE BLUE BARRELS

Checking with the principal, permission was given to use the Cafeteria stage so there would be no interference with the lunch program. Lori secured the provisions in a side room which she locked. When everything was in place she had her Basic Art classes create African designs on blue paper using the principles of design: dominance, unity, variety, rhythm, harmony, balance, contrast, proportion and a color scheme. This year she would teach the Principles of Design in a different format than usually.

When these drawings were corrected, the students enlarged them using 3 ft. by 4 ft. paper folded into grids. Matching square by square, they enlarged the small drawings to the size of the barrels. Taping the larger papers over carbon paper sheets on the blue barrels, they could trace on the African designs. When removed, they could paint the designs they had traced like the small pictures they had painted originally. They signed their names or initials and then sprayed the area with clear acrylic spray.

The blue barrels could still be seen at the bus shanties all over St. Ursula Island and the students had been made aware that the barrels were there to collect trash.

The best reward was when a student had asked if she could share a barrel with a friend because she did not think she could do it. Mrs. Artley made her do her own barrel and she DID it by herself. Later she told Lori seriously," That's the best thing I ever did in my whole life".

When all was cleaned up, the Landmarks Association honored Mrs. Artley at a luncheon, and asked if she would do it again next year. Sadly she declined due to the belligerence of some of the kitchen workers who didn't want the students to walk on their precious floors after they were mopped. They also yelled at the students and didn't want them to be in their cafeteria after they were ready to leave—two periods before school ended each day. That kind of people Mrs. Artley could do without.

Perhaps some day one of these students will develop a method for disposing of the world's refuse and solve the pollution problems. That would be really pushing the "PUSH" door!

ARTICULATING WITH BLACK HISTORY

One year when Mr. Buffalo-soldier was still a vice principal, he asked Lori on a Friday if she could have a 30' long back drop ready by Monday for the Black History program for which he was responsible and which was scheduled to be held in the gym. The wall behind the stage was 30' wide!

Of course she said, "No" since there would be no way to involve the students over the weekend. The following year when ordering supplies she put down the makings for such a back drop so that she could have one ready in case she was ever asked again. It would be hung on her longest bamboo shoot from the stand growing in her back yard. The only problem was how to get it down to school?

Mrs. Artley had her Graphic Arts class glue felt faces which they made to match their choice from a collection of great Africans and Afro-Americans which Lori had collected. They glued these felt pieces on to a roll of burlap with rubber cement. Embellishing their torsos with sequins, peanuts, gold and silver braids, fake animal furs and fabrics of all textures, this became a mural to be forever admired and hung high in the main office. The names of the figures were embroidered with contrasting yarns by the students as well as the student artist's names. In the corner, Mrs. Artley sewed a pocket in which was put a tape made by the class which told the story of each of the figures illustrated in the mural, from right to left. In that way, not only did the students in the art class learn Black History, but also, other classes which would be treated to the content of the tape by their teachers.

One of the school guards told Lori that the mural would sell for $1000.00 in New York City. Mrs. Artley gave him a snap shot so that he could see what he could do next time he was up there. The school could use the money and future art classes could make more murals.

When they finished everything, they marched it into the main office, played the tape for those present and hung the mural high on the wall which would be its home.

Several years later after the big hurricane, it needed some regluing. Mrs. Artley took it down and replaced what had blown off while another teacher, Ms. Ras, had her students varnish the bamboo pole. She played the tape for her classes and then rehung it for future generations.

Figure 44

THE BLACK HISTORY MURAL

ARTICULATING WITH SPECIAL EDUCATION

One day Mr. Odorific, a teacher of the physically challenged, dropped by and asked if Lori's Graphic Arts class would make a coloring book about the holidays on the calendar and featuring people in wheel chairs, crutches and canes. These pictures were drawn with India Ink and round tipped pens with simple, wide spaces to be colored.

This way the book would be meaningful to his students as well as teach them the months of the year and the dates of the various holidays they celebrate. Different students selected to illustrate Martin Luther King, Jr.'s birthday, President's Day, Puerto Rico Friendship Day, Easter, Mother's Day, Veteran's Day, Transfer Day(when the U.S.A. bought their island), Halloween, Primary Day, Election Day, Thanksgiving Day, Veteran's Day, Christmas, Three King's Day, and New Year's Day with one picture repeated for a cover. They chose not to illustrate Hurricane Supplication Day and Hurricane Thanksgiving Day, (which were not on the regular Thanksgiving Day as both of them were DURING the hurricane season). They had several hurricanes in spite of these holidays. Some politician had put them on the list of holidays just to give the workers another day off, with pay. No politicians wanted to eliminate them due to the unpopular image it would give them in the next election. So the holidays continue year after year.

After Xeroxing a copy for herself, Lori gave Mr. Odorific the master sheets, so he could reproduce enough copies for his classes. This idea could be used in teaching physically challenged students other subjects as well. Almost everything could be made into a coloring book for special education students.

Figure 45

Handicapped Coloring Book

ARTICULATION WITH THE SCHOOL

Many things needed attention around the school.

The art classes lettered in Old English the names and subjects of the various department chairpersons, so that students would be able to find their offices. One time they painted pictures of books to jazz up the library windows at the request of the head librarian. Sometimes they made layouts for ads in the campus newspaper and the Journalism students sold them to various businesses or they illustrated stories and made cartoons that were printed in the school newspaper and outside publications. But the greatest acclaim that they received was by the yearbook advisors who really appreciated their help and even gave a party at the end of the year.

They illustrated the divider pages and made cartoons which were of professional caliber for the Yearbook. One of the funniest categories in the Yearbook was called "Campus Fads", and in lieu of illustrating it in pen an ink, the Graphic Arts class opted for making a montage of photos for which the class posed. Using all the fads they could think of, one of the girls let her waist long, wavy hair down her back as a picture was snapped. A student in the class told them "Just a minute" and went out, borrowed about twenty gold chains of all lengths and came back with them glistening against his brown manly chest. The hard job came when returning them to the correct students afterward. Lori wondered how he ever got the right chain back to the right student. Other students wore blue denims under their school clothes, saddle shoes and "fatty' purses" around their waists. Mrs. Artley told them if they hold on to those fads long enough, the fads will come back in style.

Dr. Tickle and Ms. Beaut, the Yearbook advisors, commended the Graphic Arts class on being the only class that contributed. The advisors were slightly disgusted with the apathy of the rest of the school but to the Arts class, it was a lot of fun.

Figure 46

THE LIBRARY WINDOWS

ARTICULATING WITH PLUMBING

The following year Mrs. Artley's classes were finally consolidated into the art section in the other corner of the campus. At last they could communicate with the other art classes and appreciate each other's projects. The only problem Lori had was that some of her classes were held in the Craft's Room where there were only four tables and the other classes were held in the next room where there were seven tables. Mr. Treetop was very laid back and gave her the go ahead to move in another table. Lori even had students sitting on high stools at the sink counter to make up the twenty-seven students that were supposed to be in each class.

In the Crafts Room, where clay was used, it was easy to plug up the sink if anyone discarded clay down the drain. They were supposed to wash off the clay in a big pot in the sink but one day somebody goofed. After trying in vain to get help from the janitor, Lori brought in her fool-proof plunger the next morning. She tried to explain what she was planning to do with it to Mr. Treetop, but from the look on his face she could see he thought she wanted him to plunge the sink. He was so tall that if he ever stood in that sink he would go through the roof. Lori's plan was for her to climb up in the sink and use her plunger to clear the drain. She finally had to show him what she planned to do and the sink was cleared.

The next project Mrs. Artley had her Graphic Arts class do was make permanent painted wood signs for various places, and one was "DO NOT THROW CLAY DOWN THE DRAIN OF THE SINK". No one ever did again.

This is one way to articulate plumbing with art.

ARTICULATING WITH CONTEST WINNING

Lori found that the students did their best work when contests were held for motivation. When a contest was being held, they would enter. One day she discovered that when the Animal Shelter held its spring poster contest, no high school students ever submitted any work so these prizes always went unwon. Mrs. Artley planned to have her students make posters the next Spring when they held that contest and of course they won. This was very good for the morale as well as lucrative for the winners and went on for several years. Some students must have bragged to some chums at other schools as they started to give them some competition in a couple of years. Lori's students still brought home the bacon but they had to try a little harder.

When the principal, Mr. Boss asked Mrs. Artley to have her classes paint giant Caribbean flowers in the windows of the cafeteria she initiated a contest among her classes, with prizes donated by the Frame Up, the art shop from which the art supplies were ordered. Even students who thought they couldn't draw participated as they enlarged their drawings using grids in groups of four students, taped them outside and painted through the plexiglas windows. At the end they all signed their names and looked forward to seeing those windows when they returned to visit the school in the future.

The Pen and Ink nature drawing contests were sponsored by the National Park Service who had the winner's drawings published in the local newspaper alongside the ranger's articles. The park rangers gave a grand prize to the winners consisting of an all-day snorkeling trip to a nearby island. The students learned to snorkel as well as having a fun day in the sun.

The best Black History portraits done were not only displayed in the library for the whole school but at the local Agricultural Fair, decorating the booth that the school sponsored. Some years the winners also won basket balls which were a coveted prize.

In every contest, the entire class always received certificates acknowledging their contributions as well as blue and red ribbons for the top winners. Sometimes the winning pictures were exhibited in the nearby Curriculum Center with a handshake from the principal when the class viewed them. Every student became a winner!

At the end of the year, it was the custom for the school to present red or gold certificates to the students with high averages. By the time they graduated, some students had folders full of them; other students were happy when they just received one.

Figure 47

GIANT CARIBBEAN FLOWERS FOR THE CAFETERIA

ARTICULATING WITH THE POLICE

One recipient of these art certificates was Matt who somehow was misguided during his first three years of high school. Thus he came in his senior year just loaded with talent but no art training behind him. Apologetically, he enrolled in the Graphic Arts class which fitted into his schedule, taking the Basic Art prerequisite course another period with Ms. Lash. Once in a while his background betrayed him, as when he used Old English capitals for a poster heading so it was hard to read. His other work was meticulous and his talent was certain. He could see why he didn't win the prize for the poster. An average poster should be read in four seconds.

Years after he graduated and hurricane Hugo had come and gone, he phoned Mrs. Artley. The certificates he received had been blown away, and he NEEDED them to get the job he wanted. He was working as a detective for the police department and wanted the job of sketching suspects from witness descriptions. Lori had seen some of his work in various exhibits about town and he was very good at pencil portraits. Though retired then, she still had some empty certificates in her files and filled them in to duplicate those he had gotten years before. She was sure he would make a good police artist.

This is how art studies articulated with police work.

ARTICULATING WITH CARTOONISTS

The students always enjoyed cartooning which articulated with story writing as well as the very lucrative vocation of becoming a syndicated cartoonist. Lori told them about Charles Schultz making twelve million dollars per year for "Peanuts". Ms. Lash had loaned Mrs. Artley a terrific teaching packet on cartooning. Xeroxing this for each student, it taught the rudiments of cartooning and made the subject very enjoyable. Nobody ever said, "I can't do it". "Can't" was not a word in the art room.

At the culmination of the project, the assignment was to do a four segment original cartoon. After accomplishing this several students asked how to get syndicated.

Sometimes Lori published the student's cartoons in a stapled booklet using colored ditto masters. Other times, she submitted student works to the school newspaper or various local shopper type magazines which would print them. "All one had to do was write down all the funny situations that occur each day in school and there would be more than enough ideas to do a daily cartoon. It would be a fun kind of a vocation," Mrs. Artley thought.

ARTICULATING WITH PAINT MIXING

Oh, what Van Gogh would have done to be in these classes! He really needed Mrs. Artley's paint mixing classes after he painted his mother's face green.

By learning the color wheel the students learned that opposite colors would dull each other, and white mixed with each color lightens it, just as black darkens. They learned how to mix blue and yellow to make various greens; red and yellow to make oranges; and blue and red to make violets, as well as all the other in between colors. All the color mixing filled a booklet which each student made, with a water color picture on the final page. If time, the classes would complete another water color picture combining several reference pictures. These were matted and displayed. Some of these turned out to be very professional. The students could use paint mixing throughout their lives when mixing paint for the walls of their houses, if not for painting pictures.

One time a man who owned a paint company came to Lori's house with two five-gallon drums of paint in the back of his station wagon. He could not match the sample color his client had given him. Lori took one look and told him he needed to add the complement of the color to dull it. When he did this and mixed it in thoroughly, it matched.

Figure 48

Scratchboard

ARTICULATING WITH PHYSICAL EDUCATION

When time permitted, Mrs. Artley would end the year exposing the art classes to scratchboard. All the students loved scratchboard because mistakes could easily be covered. It consisted of cardboard covered with a thin layer of clay and then painted with black ink. When a line was scratched in it with a stylus, the line came out white. It was great to show shadows and shading. It worked well doing animals with the lines simulating fur and exotic textures. Minimal drawing created highlights from the moon. Sometimes scratchboard was used to illustrate stories read in the English classes, with press type below them quoting the line from the story.

Most students achieved success with this medium, as well as developing finger dexterity, since they had to modulate their touch. A heavy hand would cause the stylus to dig holes in the cardboard. This ability to modulate the pressure of fingers and the use of a tool articulated art with physical education as well as prepared many a student for the jobs that they would someday acquire, such as glass cutting, machine working and candy making.

ARTICULATING ART WITH THE OLD AND NEW MASTERS

When the Curriculum Center was new, unlimited Xeroxing was allowed to the teachers. Printing up single pages of pertinent facts plus some paintings to illustrate the points, Mrs. Artley made sets of Xeroxed Old Masters sheets which she passed out to her classes so they could read them together. With larger color prints she would point out things to the students, letting them keep the smaller sheets for reference as study sheets for their finals. Most students seemed to appreciate this connection with the "outside world" and returned their xeroxed papers after the finals so that she could use them the following term. Later on the classes drew a time line, so they got the approximate dates in the correct perspective. They could see the relationship to their other studies.

Since most of the Old Masters were caucasian and most of the students were negroid, Mrs. Artley considered it imperative to add the series of ten Afro-American artists of note. These artists developed after the late 1800's and a series of 20" x 30" prints of their works was offered by a company from which she ordered art supplies. When she received the "New Masters", they also enclosed one page biographies on each artist, so Lori included that in her art program for the spring term, and the Old Masters were studied in the fall. The students put them on the time line: Duncanson, Tanner, Woodruff, Laurence, Pippin, Lee-Smith, Crite, Bearden, Alston and to make ten, Mrs. Artley added in Richard Hunt, America's foremost metal sculptor who was also Afro-American. In one of her classes, there was a student whose last name was Hunt, and it became clear that he decidedly identified with Richard Hunt. He became an outstanding art student and suddenly had great interest in everything they did.

BLACK ARTISTS

Print the last name of each artist, and the title of the picture, and the mood that it creates on answer sheet provided).

10 BLACK ARTISTS
Alston
Tanner
Duncanson
Laurence
Crite
Pippin
Bearden
Lee-Smith
Woodruff
Hunt

(1) Title ---- Artist ---- Mood ----

(2) Title ____ Artist ____ Mood ____

(3) Title ____ Artist ____ Mood ____

(4) Title ____ Artist ____ Mood ____

(5) Title ____ Artist ____ Mood ____

(6) Title ____ Artist ____ Mood ____

(7) Title ____ Artist ____ Mood ____

(8) Title ____ Artist ____ Mood ____

(9) Title ____ Artist ____ Mood ____

(10) Title ____ Artist ____ Mood

Figure 49
Black Artists Worksheet

Years before, Mrs. Artley had attended an exhibit that Hunt and Bearden had shared in the Museum of Modern Art in New York City. She still had the booklets, so drew much of the information from them. She told her classes of what she had seen in that exhibit and these two artists became alive to them. At that time, both were alive and millionaires, and Romare Bearden had his headquarters at the nearby island of St. Marten.

Rounding it off to an even ten, she could use this as a unit on the final exam. She made the students aware of the artists, one of their works and what the mood or message was in the painting or sculpture. Many of the messages the artists projected in their works could be useful for the rest of the student's lives.

When she retired, she left the set to the school, as ordering them was so unreliable that they would probably never get another set. Lori felt that these works should be available in all schools and art appreciation should be mingled into the studies of the regular art classes, rather than be isolated in a class of its own.

This is how the art class articulated with the Old and New Masters.

ARTICULATING WITH MAP DRAWING

One day when Mrs. Artley was moving her class to a different location, she drew a quick 3-dimensional map of the campus and tacked it on the door. It showed where the class would be. By chance the principal saw it and asked if she would draw one like that for the whole school, to be distributed to freshmen each fall. The only school map in existence was quite outdated, so she decided to do it.

After drawing it in two different versions, she Xeroxed it down to 81/2 x 11, so it would fit on a page in the new handbook. That year newcomers to the school could find out where their classes would be.

Mr. Boss posted one of the large versions of her map right outside his office, so he could show parents exactly where the office of the department or guidance advisor they wanted, was.

A few years later, the school assigned various spots each class was to go when they had a fire drill. They then asked the Drafting Class to add the arrows onto her map. Unfortunately they did it on the small page-size map, rather than the large version, which would have given a smoother line when reduced. A copy of their new map was then posted in every classroom with the two Drafting student's names printed across the middle in bold face lettering. They had been Mrs. Artley's former students so their lettering was perfect, but they should have put their names smaller and at the bottom of the map and the year of the updating, along with the original map date.

While they articulated with map drawing, they didn't teach their students about perjury.

Figure 50

Map on the Door

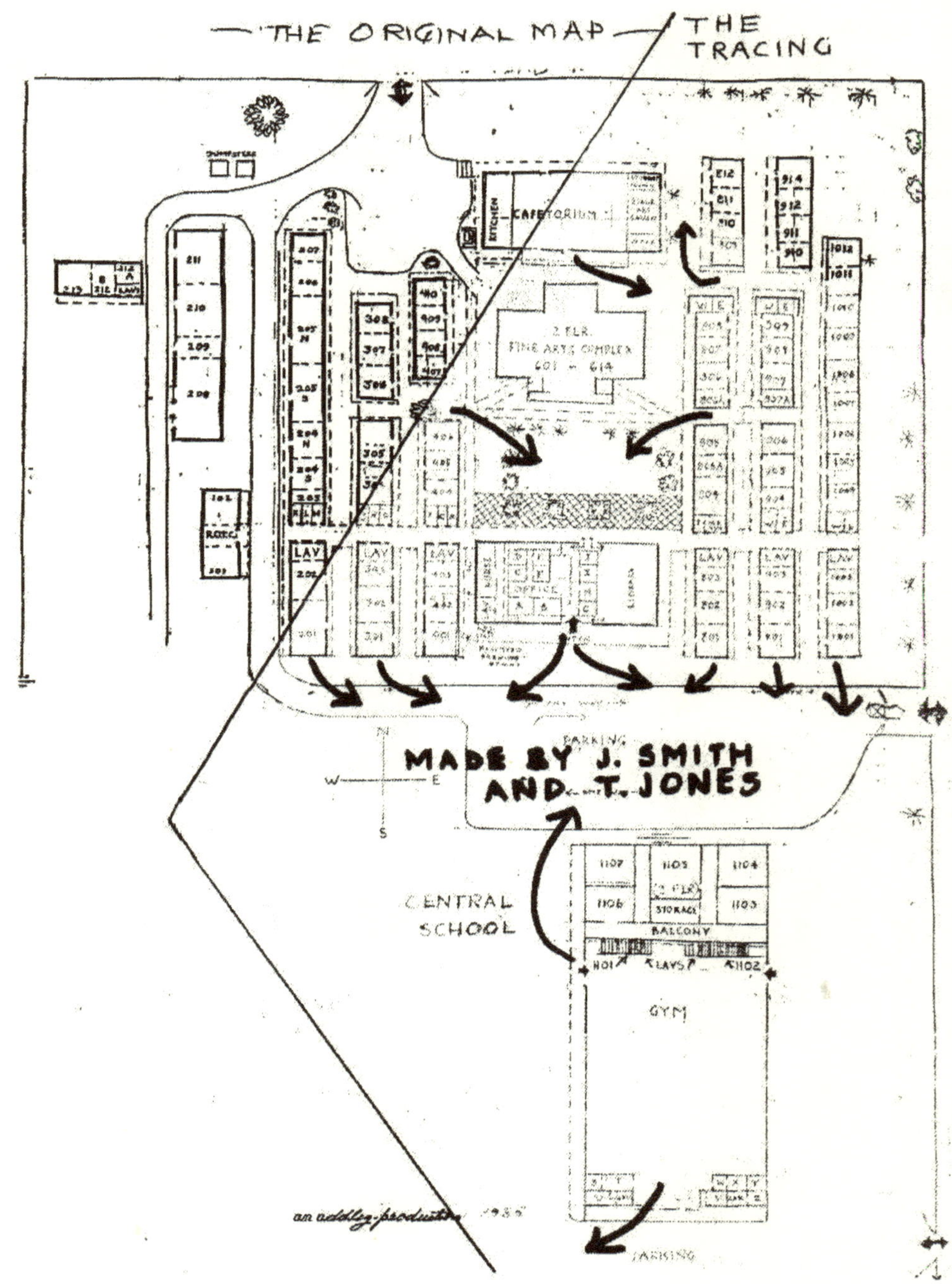

Figure 51

School Map

9

MARCHING ON

(or celebrations, parades and assemblies)

Throughout the school year, days were set aside for various celebrations, parades and assemblies which came along. The teachers felt there were too many of these and not enough time for teaching. No one listened. For each occasion teachers were put in charge of the many preparations.

The biggest one that was ever held was the Diamond Jubilee Parade which celebrated the seventy-fifth anniversary of the day St. Ursula Island became part of the United States. Preparations started months ahead with Ms. Sorority, the one female vice principal, in charge. Regular classwork was stopped in Mrs. Artley's classroom and everything centered around lettering 500 pennants, both front and back, sprinkling them with glitter, collecting sticks on which to staple them and storing them until the big day came when they would be given out to the paraders.

Ms. Sorority had the gigantic task of coordinating the entire school and involving the students so they would make a good showing in the parade. Other islands were sending as many students as wanted to come, so Central wanted to have at least the same amount, but theirs didn't get FREE boat trips.

Central also had to come up with a float behind which their students would march, including cheer leaders and flag girls. The school wanted to have a marching band also, but due to the last hurricane, the band was lucky to be able to play, sitting down...much less march too. The band leaders decided they would sit at the reviewing stand and play the school song when their fellow students came into sight.

The Art Department, beside making the 500 pennants, also were asked to make a 15 foot banner to be carried with the school name and emblem. Ms. Sugarmill had to secure a truck with a flat bed and get it decorated. She had to hold a queen contest and groom the winners to stand on the flat bed while the truck was moving. Most of the teachers cooperated as best they could, but a few tried to become invisible, not even planning to march or attend the festivities. They considered it a "day off".

Those who had to buy things kept the receipts and were promptly reimbursed. That was the first time that anything was "prompt" on St. Ursula Island.

The day before the parade, no students would commit themselves to marching. Ms. Sorority suggested that the teachers should offer bonus points to those they saw marching. Some teachers refused mainly because they didn't plan to be there themselves. Ms. Sorority made it possible for each student who marched to receive a free lunch at a school near the parade trail. Buses would take the students from Central to the parade and of course they would get pennants. The students would not be tempted. No one even wanted to wave a pennant!

The school administration held a compulsory assembly in the gym the day before the parade. The main speaker was a man from the governor's office. Every psychological argument was used on the captive audience. The school NEEDED positive public relations with the community. This parade would affirm this.

Lo and behold, the day of the parade, all the students and even the parents who helped out, wanted a pennant.

The Central students outnumbered those boated over. About 600 Central High students marched behind the banner followed by the float with the beauty queens, the cheer leaders and the flag girls followed. They were waving the pennants and marching in straight rows in the blazing sun. Lori had put a multi-gallon water cooler and hundreds of paper cups in the back of her station wagon for the students to have during their hour long wait before they marched, but the only place to park was blocks away. There was no way to get the water to them. Also, those lining them up would not want them to break ranks, because they might not be ready when they were called. The water went unused and the students bore the suffering. At least no one fainted from heat prostration.

Every school on the island participated along with the "boat people". The parade lasted for hours and all sorts of entertainers and senators got into the act. It turned out to be a great celebration!

Figure 52

DIAMOND JUBILEE PARADE

Afterwards Ms. Sorority invited all who helped, to come to her house which was near the parade path while others patronized the many nearby restaurants. The students "did the school proud". After all, if they wanted jobs after graduation, they had to see that there was good P.R. between the school and the community.

They had to be pushing the "PUSH" door that time.

——————PUERTO RICO FRIENDSHIP DAY——————

In appreciation of the many Puerto Ricans who sailed over and started small businesses on that island, when there were none in the early years, St. Ursula always celebrated to say "Thanks". Originally this was a small, underdeveloped island with few or no food, clothing or building supply stores. As a result, today one-third of the population was now of Puerto Rican descent. (Ten percent was caucasian and the rest was Afro-American.)

Due to this celebration, classes were cancelled after lunch so the students could attend a basketball game. A luncheon was set up in the cafeteria but no one from Central was invited. No publicity was in writing in the Daily Bulletin except one item which asked for donations for the Friendship Day Committee. Lori wondered each year what ever happened to all the food, donations and entrance fees collected for the basketball game.

The teachers at Central were upset by their classes always being cancelled for almost any occasion with almost no notice or input from them. Once in a while the administration would mix-up the daily schedule to keep the students from always missing the same class periods each week. But in a school with no bell system or intercoms, no one, including the teachers, could keep track of which period was what. It took "lost" students longer to reach the classes they missed so that many students just left campus in frustration. Many teachers scheduled tests or reviews at the end of the week and there never seemed to be enough time to include everything in their course. No one ever knew what was going on each day until after 3:00 P.M.

There was such a lack of communication all over campus that Friendship Day was usually a complete failure for everyone except those of Puerto Rican descent who knew the schedule. The rest of the school considered it another wasted day of pushing the "PULL" door.

Figure 53

Puerto Rico Friendship Day

——————THE HONOR ROLL ASSEMBLY——————

Over 2000 students plus their teachers usually attended this assembly each year to see who would win the honors. No one knew who was in charge, usually, since there never were enough programs and things just fell together lack-a-daisically. But then, at Central this was par-for-the-course.

Mr. Harmony was not informed to bring his keyboard, however, half-way to school he had a premonition that it would be needed so he turned his car around and went back for it. Although head of the History Department, Mr. Harmony came from a musical family and played the keyboard more expertly than anyone in the Music Department. Students and faculty alike were charmed at the celestial tones he coaxed from his keyboard when playing the school anthem in the gym. When the school finally received its classroom full of keyboards, he was asked to teach as no one in the Music Department felt adequate.

After the school had assembled in the gym, a vice principal asked Mr. Harmony to start the assembly. As if it were planned, he could play the Star Spangled Banner thanks to his premonition that morning.

Ms. Plants was always asked to decorate the stage, and she in turn asked Lori to make a permanent cloth banner which had large white letters saying "HONOR CEREMONY". This was used year after year to decorate the thirty foot background of the portable stage. One year, however, Mr. Truck had been asked to do this, so helping himself to all the colored paper rolls in the Art Office, without asking permission, he used it to cover the twelve foot by thirty foot area. Since he started late, he finished this process during the program. The department chairpersons and the vice principals sat on the stage and helped the school principal shake hands with all the recipients of the gold honor pins.

The few who had received the printed programs knew the order of events which would take place, but most of the audience including about half of those on the stage had to just watch and wait. When most had left after the ceremony, Mrs. Artley picked from the floor several programs for the use of the Accreditation Committee. Then she carefully detached all the rolls of colored paper and rolled them back up, to be stored once again in the Art Office. It had to be recycled or there wouldn't be anything left for the rest of the assemblies. Mr. Truck had disappeared as usual as soon as his decorating chores were over. He never thought about the "un-decorating".

At the end of the hectic day one of the teachers commented, "I never saw a school that tries so hard to KEEP its teachers from doing what they are paid to do!" It seemed to Lori that this school felt its job was always to push the "PULL" door.

BLACK HISTORY MONTH

The Daily Bulletin clearly stated, "at 9:20 A.M. all classes should march to the Gym with the teacher of that class, for the Black History Assembly". Though a fire drill had just interrupted all second period classes so they were behind all others, the administration chose to do it again. If they had only waited until the END of second period, at least the lesson could be finished and the students could go over to the gym on their own. Annoyed, Lori stopped teaching at 9:20 A.M. and walked her class over to the gym. The class slowly disintegrated until there were only seven members left when she arrived.

On entering the gym, Mrs. Artley noticed that no portable stage was set up, no decorations were visible and when checking with the Phys. Ed. teachers, nothing was known about the assembly in the bulletin. After exploring the huge, barn like building, Mrs. Artley went to her seven, now seated, students and told them that she was going back to her room as it was obvious that nothing was happening there. They were free to do as they wished.

On her way back, she stopped at the school office and asked, "What happened?"

It came out that Ms. Sorority had written that notice for the bulletin but the clerk-typist couldn't read her writing. Rather than question Ms. Sorority, she typed the erroneous information into the Daily Bulletin. Lori was "burned".

The following Thursday, the SAME message was printed again in the bulletin. After missing second period on Monday, Lori was not going to fall for that again. She told the class no one could leave until the booklet that was due that day was handed in. Mrs. Artley told her class, "You can leave for the gym when you have handed in your booklet". It was a good incentive to finish.

Figure 54

Black History Conference

All year long Mrs. Artley integrated Black History into her art program to make it more meaningful for her students. The usual classes were 99 and 44/100 percent Black.

The following year, a Black History Fair was held for the whole month. Teachers brought appropriate student works and displayed them in the cafeteria. The Art Department had two long tables backed with two portable bulletin boards filled with the best conté crayon portraits of famous Black people from history. On the table were ceramics and African masks from Mr. Treetop's classes, and on the front apron of the tables, Lori stapled on her ten, huge color prints of art work by the top ten black artists. She had enough posters of famous Afro-Americans artwork to staple them up across the apron of the stage. The Art Department gave a good showing.

As Mrs. Artley was putting up all this artwork, several teachers, whom she had never seen before came over and asked to borrow her stapler and scissors. Since she was using them, she declined but silently she thought it was very poor planning on their part. When unknown people try to borrow supplies, Lori found that it was imprudent to lend as she wouldn't know where to look when she needed her things back. As it was, she did loan things to teachers she knew, however when she was ready to leave, they were still using them. She had to wait til they were done because if she left, she might never get the stapler and scissors back. When things are put down for a minute, they sometimes disappear.

People who come so unprepared didn't realize what an imposition it was on those who did plan ahead. As Lori was leaving, she was asked if other departments could use the Art Department's easels. People were always ready to carry things away, but they actually forgot that they borrowed those things when it came to returning. After the Fair was over, Mrs. Artley had to comment to the teacher in charge of the Fair that each department SHOULD plan ahead and bring whatever supplies they need with them next year.

The following year the month long Black History Fair was cancelled due to the untimely death of its chairperson, Mr. Dine.

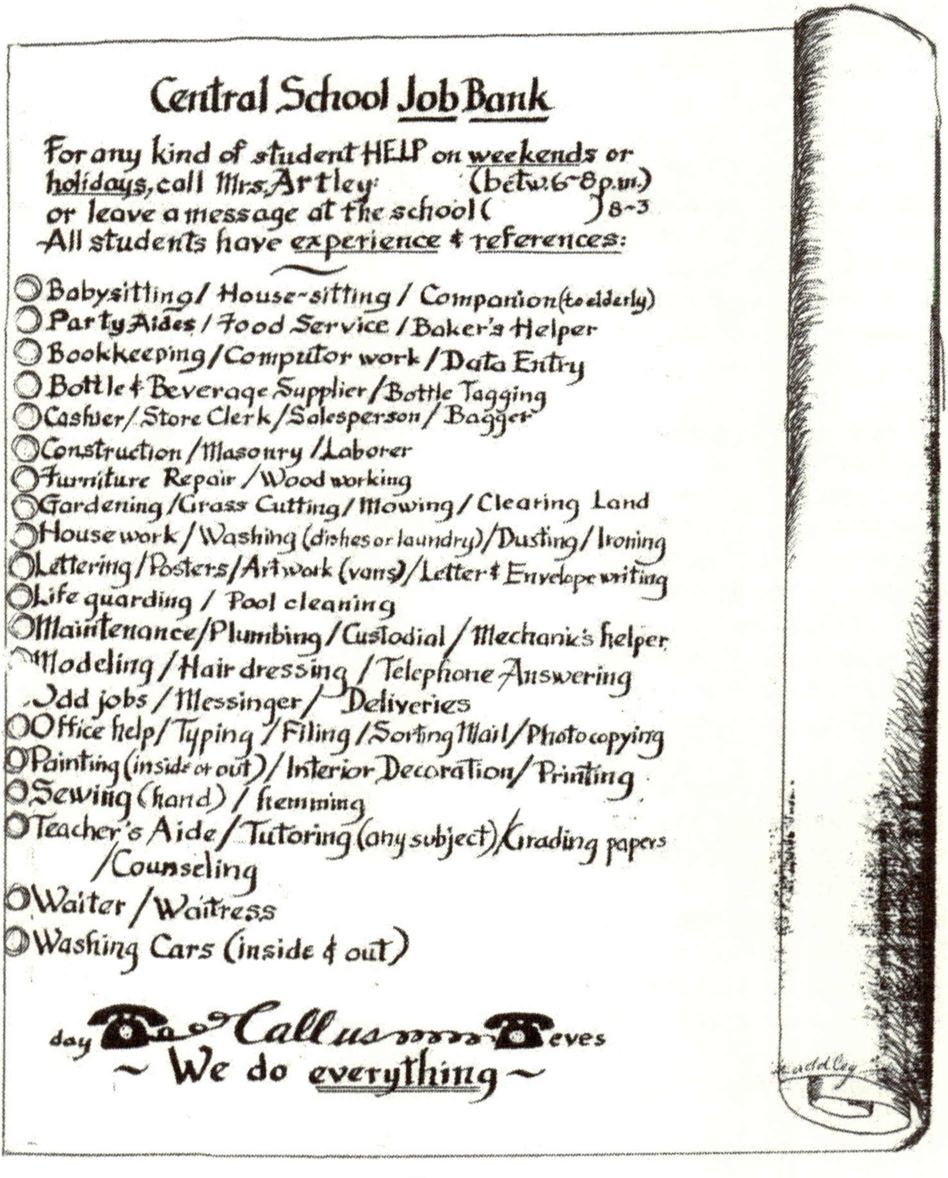

Central School Job Bank

For any kind of student HELP on weekends or holidays, call Mrs. Artley: (betw. 6-8 p.m.)
or leave a message at the school ( ) 8-3
All students have experience & references:

- Babysitting / House-sitting / Companion (to elderly)
- Party Aides / Food Service / Baker's Helper
- Bookkeeping / Computor work / Data Entry
- Bottle & Beverage Supplier / Bottle Tagging
- Cashier / Store Clerk / Salesperson / Bagger
- Construction / Masonry / Laborer
- Furniture Repair / Woodworking
- Gardening / Grass Cutting / Mowing / Clearing Land
- House work / Washing (dishes or laundry) / Dusting / Ironing
- Lettering / Posters / Artwork (vans) / Letter & Envelope writing
- Life guarding / Pool cleaning
- Maintenance / Plumbing / Custodial / Mechanic's helper
- Modeling / Hair dressing / Telephone Answering
- Odd jobs / Messinger / Deliveries
- Office help / Typing / Filing / Sorting Mail / Photocopying
- Painting (inside or out) / Interior Decoration / Printing
- Sewing (hand) / hemming
- Teacher's Aide / Tutoring (any subject) / Grading papers / Counseling
- Waiter / Waitress
- Washing Cars (inside & out)

day Call us eves
~ We do everything ~

Figure 55

The Job Bank

10

THE JOB BANK

One fall, Mrs. Artley came to school and found they had only scheduled her to teach four classes, instead of the usual five. This was because of the lack of classroom space after the big fire. Because of this extra time, Lori felt she had to use the free period to do something for the school.

Soon it became apparent that the island was in a depressed state, and that the students were hurting for money to buy school supplies. They could not even pay for lost or stolen school books. Factories and businesses all over the island were closing down leaving families without any income.

In one of her classes Lori heard two students who shared a locker, discussing their plight. The locker had been broken into and a school book costing $18.00 had been taken. J.J., one of her students, was responsible to pay for it but didn't have the money. His father had just been laid off and there were five young children in the family with no breadwinners.

Mrs. Artley broke in, asking him if he would like to wash and wax her car if she brought in all the things from home to do it. J.J. jumped at the chance. When Mrs. Artley brought in the buckets, detergent, wax and rags the next day, other students stood around watching with envy, wishing they could have the chance of earning money.

His grand finale at that job was so magnificent that she paid him $20.00. Now he could redeem the cost of the book, plus a little extra. That was the start of the Job Bank.

Students came into Mrs. Artley's room, wrote down all the jobs in which they had experience and answers to other questions on a large sheet of oaktag. Soon they ran out of space. Finally they used individual applications that Mrs. Artley dittoed for them.

One girl wanted to put down "bartending" even though she was under the legal age. The vice principal made them take that off their list. After an announcement in the Daily Bulletin, students came in during all periods for applications, and took them home for their parent's permission. The applications told their addresses and from which direction they would be taking the bus (as they were picked up for the job at the bus stop). Also there was a place for height, age, school year and which jobs they had experienced, plus two references. Many didn't know what a reference was, but they could put down personal references if they had no job experience. Some Seventh Day Adventists preferred to work on Sundays, instead of Saturdays or after school, so they circled that on the applications. Jobs did come in for every day in the week and also some for evenings and mornings.

One senior student only had two classes to attend in order to graduate. He could work any day after second period, so the Job Bank placed him painting houses.

All students were asked to obtain school insurance, as this was a school activity no matter when they worked. This came in handy when Emry pulled a brand new lawn mower backwards, cutting his army boot and part of his big toe with it. There was no "guard" on the back of the lawn mower and the blades were newly sharp. He saved the part of his toe in his mouth and was taken to the hospital where his uncle, a surgeon, sewed it back on.

He had his cousin hold down his job for him while he recuperated. Mrs. Artley visited him in the hospital and he asked her to get information about a certain musician so he could write a report for one of his classes. She looked the young musician up in the library but he was too recent to have much written about him. Instead she suggested that Emry write about Ray Charles who had led an interesting life and was old enough to have his life story written. Lori brought Emry some clippings to add to his report, so he switched to Ray Charles and wrote his report in his hospital bed.

Charlie, another student, was doing a great job but when asked how the yard work was going he admitted, "It's fine but I'm going to quit". On further examination, Mrs. Artley learned that the client, who was well satisfied with his work, always paid him by checks. He had a pile of them at home but didn't know how to cash them. Mrs. Artley called the client and they concluded that they would still pay by check but on the way to the bus stop, they would stop at a gas station which would cash them.

Charlie learned how to cash checks from this and also that checks are money.

The labor department sent over a man to see if the students were receiving minimum wages. Mrs. Artley had always insisted upon this ever since the beginning when she had heard from the students that they sometimes were paid only a dollar or two for the afternoon. She had always insisted on the minimum wage before any student was dispatched to an employer. Also the employers were to supply drinking water and any tools needed. Unless otherwise agreed, the employers also were to supply lunch, if the students worked past twelve noon. Job Bankers also sometimes received tips and presents for birthdays or Christmas when employers wished. The students had to pay the Job Bank $1.00 when joining which paid for their weekly ad in the newspaper. The ads brought in their jobs.

When clients read the Job Bank ad in the newspaper, they would call Lori at school or home. At school she had no phone, so a message went into her box and she would call from home after school. Mrs. Artley wrote to the Insular Superintendent asking for a phone to use, as her husband objected to having their home phone tied up all evening. The Insular Superintendent let her know that Lori would not get a phone and she should use Mr. Past 's phone, which was across the grass in his office. Either his door was locked or closed during continual parental conferences with students and parents. How could she interrupt these very confidential meetings to call back potential clients about a student's job? This showed Lori how <u>un</u>important the Job Bank was to the administration but it was all important to the students.

Because of this problem Lori used her home phone which was busy every night between 6 P.M. and 8 P.M. One lady mistakenly even called her at 6:00 A.M. getting her out of bed. That lady probably didn't know the difference between A.M. and P.M. as listed in the newspaper ad.

When a client called, Lori wrote the name down on an information form she dittoed. Then she looked through her file of applications for that area, and selected one which matched. She called that student, told about the job and the student called the person back and arranged to be picked up at the nearest bus stop. She or he gave the client a phone number to call, but many clients lost this and called Lori the next time to see if she knew which student they had last time. Lori wrote the student names and dates of employment on the back of the client's applications, so she could find the employer's last student. Mrs. Artley also did a lot of individual job counseling when she gave a student a job, as well as what the student should wear or bring to the job. Sometimes the student would say he/she would wear a red tee shirt so the clients would recognize him or her, and then forgot to wear it, so the two never got together. Other times students would arrive too early at the agreed meeting place, and they would keep calling Mrs. Artley as if she could do anything about their mistake. This was an annoyance. Other times clients would call Lori and spend half an hour lauding the performance of various students and what Christmas gifts they were going to get for them as they were so pleased. These were pleasant calls but time consuming.

Encouragement came from many clients who went out of their way to call or write praising letters for the students. It was one of the greatest Public Relations accomplishments the school had ever had and cost them nothing. Clients told Lori, "The girls you sent were delightful". These girls were happy to have the job of showing tour buses full of visitors the way to many "ruins" and sights on the island. They had to have two free periods in a row and were picked up and delivered to the school gate.

Another client, Ms. Yardley, who kept coming back for more students, hired one girl to clean up her old apartment when she moved. Then she hired someone to help unpack, in her new home. Then she hired two young men to paint the outside of her house. They could come at any time, whether she was there or not and earned well over a thousand dollars for college.

These two young men joined the Job Bank about a month after it had started. Mrs. Artley asked them, "Why didn't you join at the beginning?"

"Because we didn't think you'd have any jobs!", they told her. The Job Bank sustained over 200 student jobs the first school year and continually expanded.

Ms. Yardley then hired another young man to do her yard work and then an artistic young lady to take home the paints and do piece work making hand painted Christmas ornaments which Ms. Yardley sold in gift stores all over the island. Ms. Yardley was a very satisfied customer who thought the "Job Bank was a wonderful idea."

An art store hired students for yard work, grooming the company van and as sales people. The only problem: there was no bus that went that way. The boys could hitch a ride but for the girls it was more difficult. One girl walked the two miles to the store after school each day and then the owner drove her home each evening. These were coveted jobs if the students could get there.

All the male students who wanted to do yard work, got jobs. Lori could still have used more workers. Years later she met a successful young businessman carrying a brief case. He recognized her, even though he had never been in any of her classes. He told her what a wonderful experience he had had as a Job Banker and learned that he was capable of earning his own money.

Another island business man, starting his own shopper magazine, hired eight students in Mrs. Artleys Advanced Art class to come in to school on Saturdays and paste-up his magazine ads for the publication. It was good experience for them plus the pay.

One New Year's Eve, when the dishwasher for an island yacht club didn't show up for work, the frantic manager phoned Lori and asked if she could find a Job Banker to fill in at the last minute. He would pick him up at the student's house and bring him home. This turned out to be a very lucrative venture for Luther, one young man, who was a "life saver" to them.

The owners of the local do-nut shop told Mrs. Artley that they couldn't have gone to Puerto Rico for a three-day vacation if it wasn't for one of the Job Bankers who came twice a day to their house, feeding and exercising their dogs.

One time a request came in on the school phone for two "dog trainers". No student had put down "dog trainer" on the application so Lori had to resort to using the school's partial intercom which was working at the time. Teacher's couldn't call from their rooms but the office could call out. In order to use it, one had to do so at the beginning or end of the period so announcements didn't disrupt the classes. This was hard to do when one had a class to teach, but finally a free period was coming up, so Mrs. Artley raced to the office to make the announcement. On her way back to her room, two students stopped her and said they were not members of the Job Bank but they would like those jobs. They filled out applications and brought them in the next day with parental permission. They got the jobs. They told Lori that they would probably never have a job they would love more than that one.

Another time Lori had to use the intercom, was a request for a student who could type and wanted to learn the computer. It was in the bookkeeping department of a welding company which just happened to be around the corner from the home of the girl who got that job.

On the way back, Aurora, one of Mrs. Artley's own students stopped her and said, "I'm not in any typing class but I can type and I'd like to learn the computer." She was a wonderful student in class and Lori knew they would love her at the welding company. She loved the job and got to use the computer daily. She went to the job after school through out high school, over the holidays and even when she attended the local college. That was a job made in heaven.

One of the teachers at Central, Ms. Rockette, hired one of the Job Bankers to hand-sew short sleeves into all her long sleeved blouses. Long sleeves are not made for islands in the Caribbean.

Ms. Rockette also hired another student from the Job Bank to baby sit and to do her ironing. She hired two male Job Bankers to paint her whole house on the outside.

An unfortunate incident occurred there with the baby sitter from the Job Bank. Ms. Rockette noticed that one of her gold chains was missing from her bedroom upstairs. She wondered why the babysitter would have gone into her bedroom, so she put out another gold chain on top of her dresser when that same babysitter was scheduled to come. The girl took the decoy. By reporting the theft to the girl's mother, Lori got the chains back. Her mother had told her and her brother that since their true father(and dead beat dad) was not supporting them, they would have to pay for their own food and clothing. They were both under eighteen and still in school. The mother had married a new husband and he didn't feel it was his job to support other children. That is why she had to steal. How else can a young girl earn that much money? Her own mother was driving her into theft and prostitution—the very reasons the Job Bank was created to stop. Lori turned the information over to the school social worker.

One young man, Luke, who had a whole family full of over-achievers, joined the Job Bank in a very depressed state. Luke felt he could never live up to his families' expectations. To look at him, Mrs. Artley didn't think he could either, but she gave him her "best shot".

She first hired Luke to put a new louver handle on her own front door. He dropped a small screw on the ground and neither of them could find it. Fortunately Lori had saved small screws for a number of years and after searching through the drawer, they found one which would fit. Luke fixed the handle and it worked fine after that.

Lori tried to find him a maintenance job, which is what he put down on his application but they were all full-time jobs. Then a lawn mowing job came up. To make it work, Mrs. Artley had to drive Luke, after school, to his house to pick up his gas lawn mower and then half-way to the job he realized he forgot to bring the gas. Returning to his house again for the gas, she then had to take him to the job and show him the yard as the clients weren't home. Afterwards she had to come back and pick up Luke and the gas lawn mower, pay him and drive him home. The clients had left the money with her previously. He did do a good job.

Soon another client called in a request for a furniture refinisher. Since Luke had put on his application, "woodworking", Mrs. Artley asked if he could refinish furniture, too. He answered affirmatively, so she had the lady bring the furniture to his home. He looked the bedroom set over, estimating the time it would take, and gave her the price of several hundred dollars. This was completely satisfactory, and when he finished she brought him several other items to refinish. She raved over him to her co-workers and everyone who heard her seemed to have some furniture to be refinished. He had created a new business all his own and several of his clients wrote letters of recommendation to the Job Bank. One of the letters read:

Dear Mrs. Artley,

Luke completed a very large and time consuming job for me during the Christmas holidays. I found him to be an extremely personable, polite and conscientious young man. Although the work was difficult, he appeared to be more interested in whether I was happy with his work, rather than how much he was paid for it.

I am encouraging people in the community to call upon Mrs. Artley and the Central High Job Bank to find willing and able workers for their after school needs."

Luke had become a successful over-achiever like the rest of his family and a credit to the Job Bank.

When Harvey came in and joined the Job Bank, Mrs. Artley knew he would be difficult to place. He insisted on having a business job and would take no other. Finally, a company which handled the renting of villas all over the island was pleased to hire him over Christmas vacation. The company was training a new full-time permanent employee for their office and had gotten behind in their work. He helped them catch up over the holidays and this gave him business training plus a reference when he returned from college with a B.A. degree.

A man in the community was closing his electronics store and hired a young man, interested in electronics. He remained afterward to do other needed work and he was given all the electronic equipment the man no longer needed along with some electronic training to boot.

Many businesses on the island would give no longer needed items to Mrs. Artley for the school. Through her, the school received all kinds of beads from the Frame Up art store and fine rubber erasers from an architectural store which had overstocked and would rather give them to the school now, instead of after they were no good. The IRS in town donated many boxes of blank paper which their computer kept spewing out. Central High made good use of it in the art classes although Lori found it very heavy to carry out to her car and then into her classroom. The students appreciated it all and put everything to good use.

One of the most glamorous jobs the Job Bank received was a call for six T.V. technicians. A local T.V. promoter was producing a T.V. show using all the choral groups from each school on the island. The six Job Bankers were to shepherd each choral group to the right place at the right time, as well as doing other errands as they came up at the Botanical Gardens. They all had a wonderful time and wanted to do it again, even though everyone forgot to provide lunch for the group. The moral is to ALWAYS carry a granola bar with you in case of famine. The students didn't mind and only wished the jobs had lasted longer to produce the show. They all watched it on T.V. and relived the exotic experience.

Another job which the students wished to be longer was the taking inventory in Seaman's electronics store which took them the three days of a long weekend each year. It consisted of listing and counting all the items in the shop. The three girls hired for this were fastidious and especially pleased when the owner's wife took them all out to a restaurant for lunch the last day, after they finished. They learned that there was more to running a shop than waiting on customers. Also they learned to not be continually running to the ladies room to comb one's hair when they were supposed to be counting inventory.

One time a nice baby sitting job came in for every Saturday morning. Mrs. Artley called up Matilda, a student who had signed up for this category. Evidently she had forged the signature of her mother on the application and neglected to tell her parents she had joined the Job Bank. Her mother asked what the Job Bank was and though Lori had stated the baby sitting job was for Saturday mornings, she indignantly said, "You want my daughter to work on Saturday nights?" It took Mrs. Artley twenty minutes to explain that SHE didn't want Matilda to baby sit, but that her daughter WANTED to baby sit and it was for Saturday MORNINGS, not nights, and that some how her mother's signature WAS on the application. After it was all clear to the mother, she then put Matilda's father on the phone and Lori had to explain it all again. Finally, the father said, "O.K." and it all worked out fine. But Mrs. Artley was exhausted after wasting the best part of an hour. Later, when that job finished, Matilda came back with another dollar for her next job but Mrs. Artley could not afford to spend another hour on the phone with her parents explaining it all.

A souvenir business in town called up asking for three girl students: one for a bookkeeper; one for an artist; and one for a girl to do the filing and typing for every Saturday. The first thing Lori heard from them was that the owner was withholding their first month's pay—four Saturdays—in case anything was missing when they left. The Vice Principal then, Mr. Buffalo-soldier, agreed with Mrs. Artley, that this was NOT a normal business practice. Finally, the student-artist, Vivian, asked Mrs. Artley to come with her as she was quitting and wanted her last paycheck. While Vivian waited in Mrs. Artley's car, Lori had to go in and ask for her paycheck. Leaving her purse as collateral in the office, she went back to the car where Vivian signed the receipt. She then returned the receipt and retrieved her purse and drove Vivian to her home. After that, she did not supply any Job Bankers to that man but heard that the girls who remained there secured student help for the owner. A job was a job!

When Orion, a new student to Central, put down "plumbing" on his application, Lori doubted whether they would ever find a job in that category. If they ever did, could Orion do it? They did and he could.

Orion's father was a plumber and went to the jobs as Orion's "helper". They looked over the jobs, figured out the costs together and gave a written estimate. If agreeable, and it always was, they would secure the parts and return to finish the job. Orion would not only do the job for which he was hired but he would notice other things needing attention, such as if the gutters might need cleaning or if anything else needed repair. He took an interest in helping. His clients kept him coming and even told Mrs. Artley what they were buying him for Christmas. It took a lot of Mrs. Artley's time listening to his clients on the phone, raving about his fine performance. He was a winner.

One young man, Stephan, located a "dream job" when the Job Bank placed him near his home in a luxury hotel room. The owner lived right across the street but needed to "get away" from the hotel for a while, so he hired Stephan to sleep in, representing him each night and putting orange juice out in the lobby each morning. If anything went wrong, Stephan was to phone the owner and he would come over. Stephan could not believe it. He was being paid to live like a king.

J.J. dabbled in many jobs after becoming the first Job Banker. He always went home with pockets jingling, where his older brother, Don, kept borrowing J.J.'s hard earned money. The brother worked in the car wash and was lucky to come home with $4.00 for the whole day's work. J.J. looked up to his older brother who was a senior at Central, and could not say "no" to him. Finally he came to Mrs. Artley, and filled out an application in Don's name. He paid the dollar, unbeknown to Don, in order to get him a more lucrative job.

The next day, the Animal Shelter called and wanted someone to work, over the weekends, paying $50.00 each time. Lori knew that Don and

J.J.'s house was within a block of the Animal Shelter and Don loved animals, so she phoned the house and gave Don the job, much to his surprise. Even after graduating, Don stayed on full time, until he joined the service.

J.J. confided to Mrs. Artley, that he, himself, would like a job in the food service business. Up until then, the Job Bank had had no jobs in that line, but shortly after, a restaurant called, seeking a clam bar man. J.J. had no phone at that time, so Lori drove down to the nursery school where he worked and gave him the news. She had the form made out with the name of the job, the times needed, place and phone number so he called in and took the job. He liked it so much that he stayed on full time after his graduation. Eventually he went into other employment fields but always kept the "Job Bank" concept, contacting his brothers and friends who were interested in doing various jobs when he heard of them and moonlighting himself when he had time. He became a one-man Job Bank by himself.

Finally J.J.'s family were all wage earners and were able to build a little house near the one they rented. They knew it would be small at first but after they moved in, they could use the rent money to build on extra rooms which would eventually be large enough. With five boys working, that would not take too long. The depression was over.

Later on J.J. sent a bouquet of flowers to Mrs. Artley's room at Central. She called him and said, "Why now?"

J.J. answered, "When I was down town at a florist, I didn't have the money with me. When I thought about it and had the money, I was never near a florist. This time, I was in a flower shop and I did have the money!"

That Saturday, Mrs. Artley and J.J. shared a picnic lunch at Central on one of the picnic tables on the green. They talked about the Job Bank.

Mrs. Artley felt that every high school should have an active Job Bank. It teaches students the real life, practical process of earning one's own money as well as providing a legal way to earn money, rather than stealing or prostitution. It also teaches students normal business practices, such as how to cash a check; why to learn standard English; how to communicate with an employer when you cannot come; what "references" are and how to obtain them; how to fill out an application; how to be hired and keep your boss happy; how to do a full day's work for a full day's pay; how to dress for the job; how to provide the necessities of life as well as special clothes needed for the job; how to work well with others; how to estimate a job and the absolute necessity of finishing the job that you have started. It encourages young people to arrive on time, do their jobs with a smile and enthusiasm and being loyal and appreciative of their employers. It also provides an unlimited supply of willing workers capable of doing multiple jobs if only shown how.

Lori felt that students in the Job Bank were excellent public relations representatives of the school and the community needed their services. Without the Job Bank, there was very little opportunity for students to meet potential employers, and vice verse.

Through the Job Bank, a school was really pushing the "PUSH" door.

11

TROUBLE AT CENTRAL

(and Accreditation Reports)

To prepare for the accreditation team, the administration sent forms for each department to fill out and estimate its needs. At no other time than accreditation, did they ask departments to list their needs. The government didn't care what they were.

Soon after that the local newspaper headlined: "REPAIRS TO CHS COST $3 MILLION". To be precise the teachers estimated the cost of repairs to be at least four million dollars, so that the government administration could take their rumored ten per cent off the top. Since the low-bidder was always chosen, after dishing out this payola, the contractors ended up substituting shoddy materials in order to finish the job. One time the roofs and ceilings of ten English classrooms fell in on the students. Lori could see that the government plainly valued their bank accounts more than their youths.

Underneath that headline, the article stated that the Superintendent of Schools, Dr. Kreek, was now separating the "needs" from the "wants". Most of the "wants" WERE the "needs"; however Dr. Kreek told the teachers that they really didn't require this or that for accreditation and that only the "exact minimum" would be approved. This would create a façade to "fool" the accreditation committee. In case they didn't "fool" them, time would then be extended so that Central could repair a little more. In case C.H.S. never got accredited the school would still continue teaching as usual. Some schools never became accredited and didn't even try. It only made it more difficult for their graduates to be accepted by colleges. The teachers DID want their graduates to attend colleges.

An outline of the needs of Central High included: books; furniture; library equipment; an intercom system working both ways; fencing around the whole school; printing of all the outlines and committee reports, plus room and board and a grande finale dinner for each member of the accreditation committee. From where would the money come?

Figure 56

Central's Race

The Federal Government had sent educational grants with red tape tied up in the expenditures. Sometimes the local government was so confused that huge amounts were left unspent so it was sent back with the local schools still needing many things. That year $99,902.00 had been sent back so the Federal Government felt that since it wasn't spent, it must not have been needed. BUT THEY DID NEED IT, DESPERATELY!

The money should have gone to the individual schools, not to the General Fund. Each principal knew best what his or her school needed and could certainly have spent whatever money was sent...ANY amount...even if it proved too much for the island government. The individual schools could have handled it! Such stupidity tried Lori's soul!

Meanwhile at the end of each Teacher's Meeting, the Union Representative spoke for a few minutes and the principal would leave the room. The teachers would receive an update on what was really happening. One time, their Union Rep, Mr. Tailor, told them that their contract had not yet been signed, after eight months. He advised them to withhold all grades and slow down all reports and activities they were asked to sponsor.

For some reason that year the teachers received TWO W2 Forms to fill out. In a booming voice, Mr. Thin stood up and asked, "What is the REAL reason for the second W2 Form?" The real reason turned out that the government quietly planned to increase the deductions.

Another teacher complained that on the day of the great Diamond Jubilee Parade, teachers were forced to "sign in" that morning in a school near the parade, not at Central as usual. He said that he worked at Central, and that is where he wanted to sign in, but he gave away the fact that he did not want to participate in any way in the parade. Because he did not sign in at the other school, he was docked a day's pay, and Lori thought "Rightly so. He didn't do any work, so he should not have expected any pay."

The students knew that the governor had not signed the teachers contract, even though he had said several times that he would. The students had been taught that "promises made should be promises kept", and the teachers practiced what they preached. Evidently the governor did not. Lori knew that by acting in this irresponsible way he unwittingly was undermining their teaching. At one teacher's meeting the Teacher's Contract from 1923 was passed out to those present. The teachers realized that they had come a long way since 1923.

Teachers Contract 1923

This was a standard contract used throughout the Country including Wisconsin.

This is an agreement between Miss ____________, Teacher, and the Board of Education of the ______________School, whereby Miss_____________ agrees to teach for a period of eight months, beginning Sept. 1, 1923. The Board of Education agrees to pay Miss __________ the sum of ($75) per month.

Miss ______________ agrees:

1. Not to get married. This contract becomes null and void immediately if the teacher marries.
2. Not to keep company with men.
3. To be home between the hours of 8:00 p.m. and 6:00 a.m. unless in attendance at a school function.
4. Not to loiter downtown in ice cream stores.
5. Not to leave town at any time without the permission of the chairman of the Board of Trustees.
6. Not to smoke cigarettes. This contract becomes null and void immediately if the teacher is found smoking.
7. Not to drink beer, wine, or whiskey. This contract becomes null and void immediately if the teacher is found drinking beer, wine, or whiskey.
8. Not to ride in a carriage or automobile with any man except her brother or father.
9. Not to dress in bright colors.
10. Not to dye her hair.
11. To wear at least two petticoats.
12. Not to wear dresses more than two inches above the ankles.
13. To keep the schoolroom clean
    a. to sweep the classroom floor at least once daily.
    b. to scrub the classroom floor at least once weekly with hot water and soap.
    c. to clean the blackboard at least once daily.
    d. to start the fire at 7:00 so the room will be warm at 8:00 a.m. when the children arrive.
14. Not to use face powder, mascara, or paint the lips.

Because of unionizing, the teachers had been able to not only improve working conditions but also to upgrade the teaching profession for the benefit of the students. All kinds of new innovations were happening in all schools. This could not have been possible without unionizing.

The next teacher's meeting produced a new report by the union rep. It seems that the governor had LIED each month and now came right out with the truth. He now would NOT sign the contract. They voted unanimously to STRIKE.

The marking period was ending the following week and they agreed to not even figure up the grades or record them anywhere. They also would not cooperate with any activities and would hold a general slow-down. They were told that lesson plans and accreditation reports could be written out but not handed in. Departments which were to report at the weekly accreditation meetings should say they were not yet ready. No one should ask any questions or submit any additions if any reports were read:

FEDERATION OF TEACHERS

SLOW-DOWN LISTING OF EXTRA CURRICULA ACTIVITIES

TEACHERS/PARAPROFESSIONALS

DEFINITION: EXTRA CURRICULA ACTIVITIES—ALL ACTIVITIES OUTSIDE YOUR REGULAR CLASSROOM INSTRUCTIONAL DUTIES.

LIST OF DO'S:

*SIGN IN
*SIGN OUT
*PERFORM REGULAR INSTRUCTIONAL DUTIES
*PARAS REMAIN ON YOUR POSTS
*PREPARE LESSON PLANS
*TAKE ROLL & ATTENDANCE

LIST OF DON'TS:

*ATTEND FACULTY MEETING
*FUND RAISING SALES
(CONTRACTUAL ½ HOUR)
*GRADING OF CARDS
*FIELD TRIPS, FAIRS, WORKSHOPS
*ASSEMBLIES/PROGRAMS
*SUBMISSION OF DETENTION FORMS
*VOLUNTEER COMMITTEES/CLUBS
*MAY POLE
*SPORTS DAY
*ATTEND PTA MEETINGS
*FUN DAY
*TUTORIALS
*CAFETERIA SUPERVISION
*TRACK MEETS
*CURRICULUM CENTER TRIPS
*MATH BEES
*SCHOOL IMPROVEMENT TEAM MEEETINGS
*RECESS DUTIES
*PURCHASING EXTRA SUPPLIES
*HALL MONITORING
*TRANSPORTATION OF STUDENTS
*HOMEWORK HOTLINE
*AFTER SCHOOL PRESENTATIONS
*COACHING
*SCHOOL ACCREDITATION COMMITTEE MEETINGS
*OUT-OF-POCKET EXPENSES

At the next accreditation meeting, they finished fifteen minutes ahead of schedule, because of this policy. To kill the time, the vice principal went over the next day's schedule: It seemed that because seventh period had been skipped so many times it would be put at the beginning of the day, skipping first period instead. From there they would go backwards, to six and so on until the afternoon which would be a Talent Show held in the gym as a fund raising event.

As the changing bell could not be heard in most of the classrooms, this schedule predictably led to mass confusion. It had not been published anywhere, nor was it printed up on a poster with the changing times listed. Most classes had the wrong students in them and little or no learning was accomplished that day. Even the administration, who should have learned by now not to mix up the schedule, didn't know what time it was. But then they were always pushing the "PULL" door anyway.

"One can easily understand why kids don't learn in this type of school", Lori mused. As a fitting end to one teacher's meeting, Mr. Thin went wild, yelling in a high squeal, "When will you ever learn?"

When they finally could see that their "slow down" was not achieving its goal, there was no alternative but to strike at the end of the year. The administration probably thought the slow down was "normal".

The union filed for "Strike Action" and they were asked to turn in all classroom keys. Most of the keys were the property of the teachers who had them copied from another teacher's key, as there was such a disorganized method of keeping track. In order to continue receiving their paychecks the teachers handed in "dead" keys marked with their room numbers when they left. These keys were from old houses, cars, trunks...anything but the right ones.

To start the strike off right, the teachers formed a motorcade, starting at the farthest schools and ending up at Government House. The teachers from each school joined the motorcade as it passed. The huge numbers of cars then on the road cut off most other traffic. When they neared Government House, they parked at the nearby Union Headquarters and marched with giant placards down to Government House. Speeches were heard and refreshments made available, but nothing great was accomplished. The end of the term came, and the student's projects were unfinished with no time to review for final exams. The term ended on a low note.

That summer the teachers entered into binding arbitration with the governor, and won. The mediator decided that since the governor's representative had accepted the contract the summer before, the governor had to honor it also. This was so simple! During all this time the newspapers were full of letters from parents, teachers and students, all in favor of the teachers.

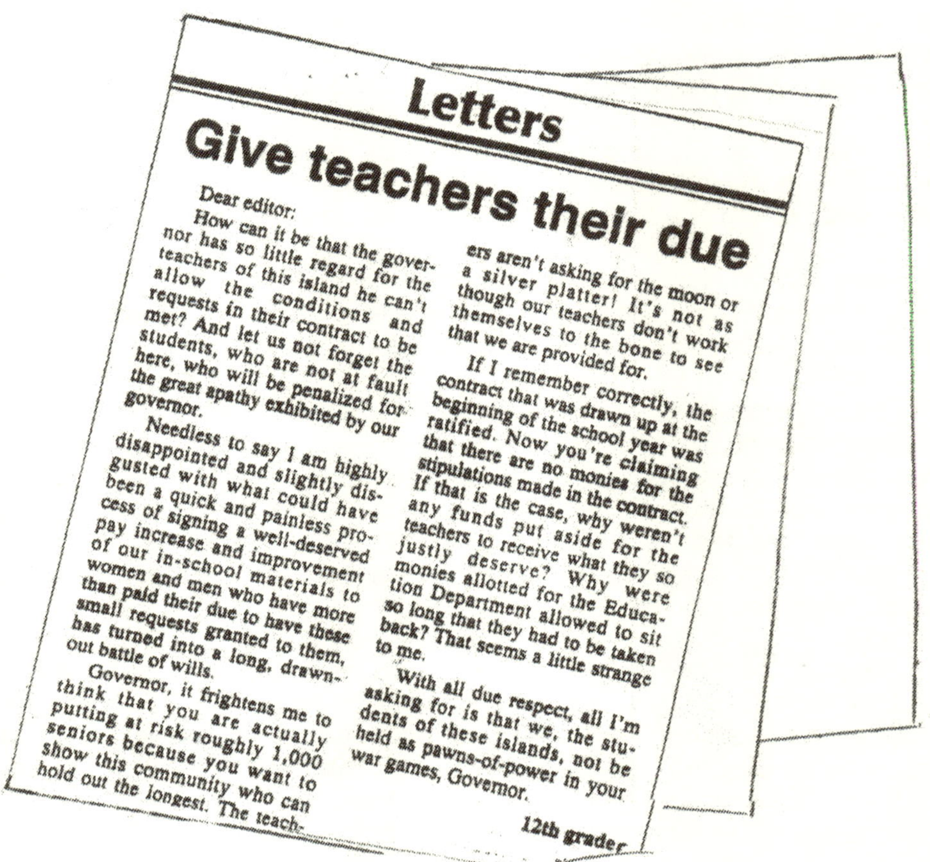

Letters

Give teachers their due

Dear editor:

How can it be that the governor has so little regard for the teachers of this island he can't allow the conditions and requests in their contract to be met? And let us not forget the students, who are not at fault here, who will be penalized for the great apathy exhibited by our governor.

Needless to say I am highly disappointed and slightly disgusted with what could have been a quick and painless process of signing a well-deserved pay increase and improvement of our in-school materials to women and men who have more than paid their due to have these small requests granted to them, has turned into a long, drawn-out battle of wills.

Governor, it frightens me to think that you are actually putting at risk roughly 1,000 seniors because you want to show this community who can hold out the longest. The teachers aren't asking for the moon or a silver platter! It's not as though our teachers don't work themselves to the bone to see that we are provided for.

If I remember correctly, the contract that was drawn up at the beginning of the school year was ratified. Now you're claiming that there are no monies for the stipulations made in the contract. If that is the case, why weren't any funds put aside for the teachers to receive what they so justly deserve? Why were monies allotted for the Education Department allowed to sit so long that they had to be taken back? That seems a little strange to me.

With all due respect, all I'm asking for is that we, the students of these islands, not be held as pawns-of-power in your war games, Governor.

12th grader

Figure 57

The Letters

Everyone was delighted to get rid of THAT governor at the next election.

The following fall, the school administration became jealous of the teacher's strike, and held a "sick out" for themselves. Everyone wanted to get in the act!

Coming in early that "sick out" day, Mrs. Artley had planned to use the ditto machine. Instead, on arrival she was informed that there was a teacher's meeting currently going on in the library. It was nice to know about these meetings so far in advance!

Upon arrival in the library Lori learned that the five administrators had all called in "sick" in protest to the demand that they work twelve months per year, less vacation time. They would be compensated by a 1.5 % raise in their already elevated salaries. The teachers decided that since the administrators had never shown any support during their strike, they would do likewise. If any individual teacher wished to show support, s/he merely had to "sign out" for the day on a list at the front desk.

One worry wart of a teacher spoke up, "What if the students get into a fight that day? Who will be responsible?"

"The monitors would handle it as usual. Just wait and see." Over the intercom which now covered only the office and the library, it was announced that their former principal, Mr. Boss, would be arriving at school to take charge for the day. He was now the Assistant Commissioner of Education.

That day went better with the five administrators out than when they were present. There were no fights. Everyone felt, "Who needed the principals?" They were always pushing the "PULL" door, anyway.

ACCREDITATION REPORTS

Central High School was coming up for accreditation at the end of the year. It could be postponed, if not ready or if CHS couldn't become accredited. The team would extend their time until the school was "fixed up" according to their recommendations. Many of the recommendations which they made at the time of the last accreditation, were still not achieved. If CHS at least showed progress toward attaining them, they would extend.

That same week they asked Mrs. Artley to become department chairperson. Mr. Buffalo-soldier gave her three accreditation reports for the Fine Arts Department saying, "they should have been handed in two months ago" as if it were her fault. Every night that week Lori sat at typewriter filling out forms to the best of her knowledge.

One of them she couldn't understand at all. It was to list everything the Fine Arts Department needed and state who could supply this and how much it would cost, plus installation, shipping and handling. Lori had to make an appointment with him and ask what she should put down. His answer was "guesstimates" as these papers were two months overdue and he said, "they will not approve any expenditures for the Fine Arts Department, anyway". He then explained that Fine Arts was the smallest department in the school and therefore not important. Mrs. Artley countered by stating that Fine Arts was the MAIN department for achieving GOOD publicity for the school, as students were taught to perform instrumentally, vocally and artistically throughout the community. The only other department which made its student's prowess known to the community was Physical Education. They got plenty of funding!

Figure 58

ACCREDITATION REPORTING

Later on when Mrs. Artley's department learned that she had submitted the three overdue reports without their input, they acted annoyed, like she should have called meetings including them. Why didn't the previous chairperson do this? They were two months overdue! Whenever meetings had been called, they were always "too busy" and they wouldn't stay after 3:15 P.M. even though they were paid for an eight hour day. Their lunch periods didn't match, so that was out. They had to cancel class periods for meetings, and teaching classes was their job.

As luck would have it, Mr. Buffalo-soldier was "removed" that summer and the new principal couldn't find most of the accreditation records and reports, so everything had to be done again over the next school year anyway.

The following school year, the teachers came to the accreditation meetings, filled out the pages necessary and gave their input without the grumbling and excuses as in the past. They handed everything in on schedule and Lori retired at the end of June.

The school needed to have the time extended anyway and everyone still had to fill out yet another set of accreditation reports again that next year. The ratings were too low to get them accredited.

Usually accreditation meetings were held the last period each week, and the departments were expected to read aloud each question and answer in their report booklets.

Often these meetings were held during Activity period, which meant the students were left to wander aimlessly, unsupervised. Only the monitors were left to "watch", but often they were not where the action was. Fights took place during this free time, some of them planned beforehand as amusement for the crowd that always gathered.

One time the students were sent, bloodied and stabbed, to the local hospital and sixteen students were hauled into the principal's office. At this exact same time the Accreditation Team was arriving at the airport, and the head monitor, Mr. Moresum, was unable to greet them as he was busy capturing the students. A lead pipe was confiscated but the knife was never found. The next day, the front page of the newspaper carried the whole story for the Accreditation Team to read, as they prepared to evaluate the school.

Students often came to school bearing guns, knives, scissors, drugs and lead pipes in their knapsacks. Several times searches were held in the cafeteria, but many students deposited their weapons in bushes on the way so they would not be found.

The mischief unsupervised students devise, beside the fighting, was pure vandalism. They would take anything not attached to the buildings as well as some of the things that were. Anything merely attached would "walk off". Even the hinges above certain doors and "EXIT" signs disappeared. A student was rarely seen studying or doing homework while the teachers had to attend accreditation meetings.

Years later Lori was on jury duty with one of her former but well-to-do students. She asked him why he had chosen to attend Central instead of the several private schools on the island. He replied in all candor, " I knew that if I made myself learn at Central, I would have a better chance in college, as there is no one to prod you and all the deterrents are still there. Central DOES have some excellent teachers, so if you WANT to learn, you CAN".

For accreditation reports, all the teachers squashed into the small library, as it was the one meeting area with air-conditioning. About one-fourth of the teachers had no chairs, so sometimes Lori brought her own. After the report was read, the group could ask questions or give additions or criticisms, if there wasn't a "slow down" at that time. Usually three reports could be read in one day.

During one of the slow downs, Mr. Mountain was in charge of the meeting. Each department scheduled to read that day stated "it wasn't ready yet". Mr. Mountain countered by making everyone stay there until three o'clock in silence. Not being able to waste time doing nothing, Mrs. Artley asked for permission to leave for necessary functions, and returned with some papers to grade. Why waste time doing nothing when there was so much to do?

When the Fine Arts Department read its report, the principal commented that all answers were so negative. He was told that honestly, the department had received no supplies in over five years. Also smaller classes were needed, so that individual time could be given to each student and the students were not "screened" by the counselors to make sure they were interested in learning art or music. Often, Mrs. Artley observed, that students were put in art classes for disciplinary reasons or because there was no room left in the typing classes. The last accreditation, ten years previous, had recommended these changes, but C.H.S. had never even tried to accomplish them.

Due to this, several teachers decided to meet with the principal privately. Asking for an appointment before school began, they arrived at 7:25 A.M., the time he had stated. He told them that he couldn't meet then as he had to do the "payroll docking" because of his deadline. HE postponed the conference until after lunch at 1:30 P.M.

When they returned at 1:30, he was not on the school grounds. One of the teachers there said she had seen him drive away at 1:29. Mrs. Artley resolved to just sit there until he came back. The others in the group went to meet their classes. This was typical of the way Mr. Buffalo-soldier treated the teachers. Even during a meeting in his office he would make phone calls or do other private work. He would not listen to what was being said.

When he finally returned at 1:54 P.M. Mrs. Artley sent for the other teachers involved in the meeting. He didn't mind docking the payroll of teachers who didn't attend HIS meetings, but he made no apologies or excuses for not attending theirs.

As a result of this meeting, Lori volunteered to retype the Fine Arts accreditation report changing the objectionable wording but still stating the truth. As he mentioned, it was to everyone's advantage if the school became accredited.

After several postponements, the school finally became conditionally accredited several years later. Central was always pushing that "PULL" door!

12

THE EVENING YEARS

or

(Retrospect)

One should always prepare for retirement years before the actual event. A Retirement Workshop was announced in the Daily Bulletin late on the day before it was to occur. This "advanced notice" allowed many teachers to sign up to attend, including Mrs. Artley. Unfortunately the Daily Bulletin didn't get into her possession until AFTER classes were finished for the day, so there was no way to give the students an outside assignment for the next day. Lori put an explanation inside the glass window on the door to her classroom, assigning students to continue sketching in their sketchbooks for their artwork that day.

The workshop was scheduled for 9:00 A.M. at another school. It started about fifty minutes AFTER that time. First everyone had to register and receive a packet of materials. Time could have been saved if the packet had been handed out at the door as the attendees arrived. The registration sheet should have been inserted in the packet, and then collected later. Having several hundred people waiting in long lines for these two items wasted everyone's time as well creating a very boring start. Utilizing those fifty minutes would have enabled the workshop to end on time.

They were then informed that "very informal sessions" would be held until 4:10 P.M. This put a hardship on those teachers who had to pick up their children after school, exactly sixty minutes earlier than the conference ending.

In general the speakers were interesting and the information pertinent but the fact that it would take six months or more from the date of retirement to the date of one's FIRST retirement check was not mentioned. Instead, they emphasized that one should apply for retirement two years preliminary to the date. Lori did this the next day to give them the two year notice, but still had to wait over six months for her FIRST retirement check. Do they expect their former personnel to stop eating for six months? Also, the health care contribution was supposed to

Figure 59

THE RETIREMENT CONFERENCE

be paid by the retiree during those six or seven months, even without getting any paychecks.

One of the speakers of the day was a retired man who mentioned all his illnesses since retiring. At 72 years of age, he swam, sang and walked but had given up smoking. He brought up the redundancy of having to pay taxes AGAIN on his retirement checks as well as Social Security. At the end, Lori only hoped that the retirement office planned ahead more efficiently than that retirement workshop did.

Two years later, she found out they didn't.

After that workshop, Mrs. Artley sent a letter immediately to the retirement office stating her intentions. Two months before retirement, she submitted a letter of resignation so they could begin her paper work. Mrs. Artley mentioned that she would like to retain her health plan after retirement, but evidently that vital information was not passed on.

When she tried to get her health plan in place she found that the health plan official's job was a political plum, and that person in charge was usually not there. That woman never informed her that her letter was not enough and that she had another form to be filled out. Lori figured they would continue to take money out of the retirement checks to continue the plan, as they had done with her previous pay checks, even though they weren't paying her yet. Evidently that was not the case and no one informed her until they cancelled the policy. Realizing this, she had to go through a lot of red tape, many phone calls, letters and send checks to cover the cost for several months until the company was finally convinced that this was all a comedy of errors.

The person who handled her records in the government office hated to go into her files because they were so mixed up. Lori had a six inch pile of duplicate letters she had written trying to straighten the whole mess out. Mrs. Artley figured out that this is what occurs when political appointees, who have no training in the necessary field are given government jobs because someone in their family worked to get votes for the ruling party.

She felt it was certainly ironic that this island government expected its retirees to shell out money to pay the cost of its health plan when no pay checks were being paid to that person for over six months.

This goes on year after year, even though it is a very unrealistic approach and many retirees suffer. After surviving all of this Lori surmised that the only conclusion to be drawn was: NEVER RETIRE!

Figure 60

THE CENTRAL SCHOOL EXPERIENCE

THE CENTRAL SCHOOL EXPERIENCE

We all have heard about the "Black Experience". Well, there are other experiences also, like the Central School Experience.

The Central School Experience has happened in all schools and was many different things to many different people. It was certainly like no other experience.

One teacher told Mrs. Artley that after a day of teaching at Central she had to go home to bed and have perfect silence for three hours before she could pick up the pieces again.

Teachers have different experiences than students, administrators, staff and parents. All have different experiences. It stems from how everyone affects others.

It is the feeling a student at Central got when he was informed by a Vice Principal that he could not pay for his stolen text book except between the hours of 10 and 11 A.M. in his office. Mr. Lackley felt he was "toughening up" the students for later life. This reminded Lori of the "toughening up" of a pet dog which she witnessed in Puerto Rico. Bound with a rope around his neck, the ten year old boy threw his trusting pet ten feet down from a pier into choppy ocean water, forcing him to swim until exhausted. Lori called that cruelty... not toughening up! In the same sort of case on St. Ursula Island, a man tried to toughen up his pet ram. One day the goat had had enough and he butted the man into a fence and killed him. Mrs. Artley felt that was justice served.

Another Central School experience was when Lori learned that a student in her homeroom was being given a failing grade in Agriculture because he did not have the money to buy a wool blazer with an emblem on the pocket. He could only wear such a jacket if he attended an agriculture conference in the states. He said, "There's no use for a wool jacket on this island which was between 80 to 90 degrees in temperature all year around". Students who didn't buy the jacket, through their teacher, failed the course and very few had money to attend conferences in the states.

Everyone who entered the Central School gates had the feeling of "losing touch" with the outside world as there were so few telephones-in-working-condition. In an emergency, Lori had once asked the head librarian to let her call out. She was allowed to use the library phone because, the head librarian said, "I know you won't ask again." Lori didn't.

The Central School Experience was also the knowledge that a teacher might never return home again after school due to the violence, destructive threats, drugs and weapons.

Mrs. Artley's Central School Experience included being told by a paid employee, "This school doesn't need old, white teachers, like you." Even though he ate his words later when Lori repainted four outdoor signs after her retirement. He realized she was missed. They did need "old, white teachers" like her.

Central was always short of teachers and had to make receptionists and aides teach classes. Even people off the street who had no teacher training could get jobs teaching at Central if they wanted to teach the right subjects.

Lori's Central School Experience also included being "cussed out" by that English teacher with whom she shared a room. Then she experienced the teacher lying and using vulgar language. At the end of the school year, that English teacher apologized as she had since found religion. Lori hoped she held onto that religion because she really needed it badly.

Also, Lori's Central School Experience included students who threatened her when they didn't achieve a passing grade, and then did damage to her car. Did they think they could get away with that all their lives?

The Experience also included never hearing the outcome of reports sent in to administrators. Although teachers were always expected to send in reports, they rarely got any feed-back.

Lori's Central School Experiences included rudeness on the part of various students, undoubtedly incurred to delay the lesson, or throwing fire-balls in the classroom...even burning down an entire building of twelve classrooms. When others are rude, one can only assume that they come from that kind of a home.

Lori's 'Experience' included seeing workers mow down young trees, cacti and flowering bushes which were planted by caring teachers to beautify the campus. Sometimes dug up and stolen or crushed by careless workers throwing sheets of plywood down on top of them, the whole life of such people must be one big void.

Lack of caring showed up all over campus. Doors without locks, broken key holes stuffed with debris and paint slopped over numbers to rooms shows lack of supervision and no knowledge of "know how".

It took a long time to get over students tip-toeing behind her back as she typed and stealing a plexiglas show case displaying student works. All non-essential items. The thief would steal rather than buy the contents made by other students who were trying to sell them.

The 'Experience' included planned fights to keep classes from starting—the students circled around egging them on.

One of the students in the hospital with a seven inch gash in his side said, "The first thing I am going to do when I get out is retaliate". It is virtually impossible to expel the perpetrators of these crimes due to all the red tape, documentation and public hearings involved.

When Mrs. Artley taught at a public school in Hartford, Connecticut, she found all the doors chained shut after school each afternoon. She had stayed later than usual, unloading the kiln. What would have happened if one door had not been left unchained? That was another Central School Experience.

There was also a good side to Central School Experiences. Late one afternoon when her car wouldn't start, Mr. Khaki and some R.O.T.C. students helped her get it moving so she could take it to the nearest gas station. The fuel line was stopped up.

A good feeling came over her when she heard that one of her former students had raised his fists with another because he felt she was the best art teacher in the school. The vote of confidence banished the discouragement that all teachers sometimes feel.

It was a happy Central School Experience when letters of commendation and thanks were put in her personnel file at the school. Lori liked receiving the mahogany clock, plaques, pen sets, certificates and medals for her artwork which she contributed to the school. She believed and taught that artists should give of their talent to their communities. "Whatever one can do well is a gift from God and should be shared", Lori felt.

Mrs. Artley appreciated the huge Chinese urn which the school gave her on retirement and the beautiful glass paperweight her colleagues had given her when they treated her to a retirement luncheon at an island hotel. These are good Central School Experiences which Lori would always remember.

The good and the bad...these and more are happening at schools throughout the world. Sometimes Lori felt that the bad experiences were directly related to the fact that many real-life courses have been removed or never even included in the school curriculae: swimming, life saving, survival, marine biology, hygiene, sex education, physical education, driver education, music and art. These are sometimes expensive but they save lives. High School is one of the last times that a "captive" and receptive audience can be taught these real life skills en masse. Often, courses such as these are the only reason some students WANT to come to school.

Lori's good experiences included the first meeting she attended at Central held at a nearby school. Then all the teachers were supposed to go to the school in which they would be working. The Artleys only had one car at that time, and didn't know that she would have to go to the other school after that meeting, so Bill had just dropped her off, and planned to pick her up at 3:00 P.M.

She started walking the mile to Central and after she had gone about a block, a car stopped. It was a fellow teacher who was making room in his car for her. She was gratified that he was without prejudice, would pick up a caucasian teacher and had noticed in that short time that she was teaching at Central. He always was remembered for his kind deeds and though they taught in different fields, many kind thoughts came his way.

Another good experience Lori had at Central was when she and Ms. Angel would have lunch together and visit various places afterward on Saturdays. Ms. Angel showed Lori exactly where to pick up conch shells on the shores, where the fishermen had thrown them after removing the meat. Lori filled her car several times and placed them along her driveway and garden.

Another time they visited Ms. Angel's mother's grave and placed conch shells over her grave. Other days Ms. Angel showed Lori her "private" place where they could sit on a bench overlooking the turquoise Caribbean Sea and enjoy the silence together. Ms. Angel always picked herbs along the way as they went home, to give to her uncle. These times will never be forgotten.

Instead of including cheaper but irrelevant courses, schools should beef up the curriculae. On this island Mrs. Artley experienced having two of her students drown. One would think that swimming would be a compulsory course, but it was not even taught in any of the public schools!

One thing was sure, Lori felt: It will take EVERYONE to solve the educational problems—people with children and those without. After all, if children are not educated, they take to stealing out of necessity...and they steal from <u>everyone</u>. Educate all children in the things that count. Give them a GOOD Central School Experience! Show CARING!

ADDENDUM

On St. Ursula Island the governor appointed a commission on education to study the problems and come up with solutions. The commission asked the community to submit ideas and held several hearings. Mrs. Artley was pleased to see Mr. Boss, now retired, but speaking up at one of the hearings. He moved up the educational ladder hoping to solve some of these same problems. Not enough autonomy was given to the principals, and yet they were the only ones that knew what their schools really needed.

Another person who spoke up at a hearing was the first Job Bank student, J.J., now a pillar of society. Among other things he was now an Americorps Volunteer and worked with others through the Women's Coalition.

There were others at the hearings whom Lori knew and everyone had their say...but this was the governor's commission. They handed in their recommendations and nothing was done. Would the local government see that changes were made, or was it just another political maneuver?

Some of Lori's suggestions that needed to be considered were:

1. To reduce the thievery in schools, trailer homes should be placed on each campus, with responsible people living in them. This costs less and provides more protection than hired guards, who sometimes do more evil than good. The person(s) would be responsible for the school grounds when school personnel were away. It has worked at schools where it has been tried.

2. Teachers should not be asked to be present for events or decorate for dances on weekends or holidays because they usually have their own plans. Also, they should not be asked to letter certificates or make murals over their weekends. They should teach their students to do these things but not burden them with repetition. Teachers are paid to teach.

3. In each room there should be a two-way intercom from classroom to office, so that discipline problems, rape, fights, thefts and other mayhem may be reported and monitors may be sent to the spot quickly. Without this, there was no way to

receive help when needed. One time in Connecticut a fight started outside a classroom door. The teacher locked the door and then called the office. On this island that would not be possible.

4. All teachers should stay in their classrooms while students were present, except for an emergency. Without this understanding, teachers have left classes to make phone calls, to flirt with other teachers, or just to get out of teaching. While one teacher was making a phone call, a fight broke out in her class; a student was injured and the doors on a large storage cabinet were knocked off. If the teacher was being paid to teach, s/he should be in the classroom teaching when a class was there.

5. Changes in daily schedules should be announced IN WRITING a minimum of two days before the event. The announcement should be read to all the classes and the change in schedules should be posted. This would avoid chaos in schools without bell systems, saving everyone from another wasted day. The school administration should try not to disrupt the scheduled classes. It should plan to hold special events during different periods each time.

6. Every back room or staircase should be checked for lighting, and brighter lighting installed where needed. Teachers and students are ruining their eyes with the poor lighting systems in halls, backrooms, corners, teachers lounges and bathrooms in schools. Each month these places should be checked as well as including leaking water fountains, toilets and dripping sink faucets.

7. Student Services should be developed to give aid to teachers and counselors, in paper work and other functions. This will give the professionals more time for teaching and counseling, as well as teach students what is involved in these jobs. Counselors should be situated away from the main office, for easier access by students and for privacy.

8. Education should be in compliance with the Disabilities Education Act and see that there are adequate facilities for the handicapped. Physically challenged students should be mainstreamed when ever possible, accompanied by a paraprofessional if necessary. Volunteer tutors should be

organized to help where needed as well as speech, child psychologists and physical therapists available at each school. Tutors should be available to any student who wishes to have one.

9. More decision making powers should be given to those in each district and the principal of each school should have budgetary powers for her or his school.

10. Accountability for student's attendance in each class should be available each day, as well as substitutes for teachers who are absent. Academically talented classes and remedial programs should be reinstated, and volunteers from the community should be welcomed in the schools. Students should not be promoted or graduated just because they have reached "that age". They must learn and earn their grades. If they leave school before graduating, students should go to trade school or join the Youth Corps etc.

11. High schools MUST offer prevention programs to lessen teenage pregnancies. Sex education should start in Kindergarten, if not before. By the time students reach high school, they should have already decided against promiscuity. When students have goals that include further education, they are adamantly against having children before marriage. The pregnant girls and the would-be-fathers should not be kept in school with the rest of the students, as they undermine goals and try to make the other students envy their promiscuous position and eulogize them with baby showers. After the birth, the young mothers should not be allowed to bring the baby to school to show it off. If they wish to graduate, they should get a G.E.D diploma. These young fathers should also attend adult education classes rather than staying where there is the possibility of impregnating other young ladies. They definitely would be a deterrent if they return to the regular high school.

12. Any teacher requesting a paraprofessional or teacher's aide in his or her classroom should be granted this. At times, it is absolutely necessary to have two adults in a classroom.

13. Peer-teaching for teachers should be established on a voluntary basis. Any teachers wishing to learn other subjects should be

allowed to sit in on other classes during their free periods provided there is room.

14. There should be on-going curriculum development which articulates each subject with as many others as possible, whether or not the curriculum is scheduled for updating or needs to be written if it is non-existent. Progress should be monitored at evaluation time at the end of each school year.

15. There must be ongoing staff development which articulates with all grade levels in the school system. At least one conference should be held each year with each grade or subject included, so that what is being taught becomes more advanced as the student progresses into higher grades.

16. Field trips into the "outside world" should be encouraged and made possible with transportation grants and blanket class insurance for each class. The many requirements at present tend to discourage class trips which could open a whole new world for the students and give them a REASON for learning. They can see how their subjects interrelate with the community.

17. Teachers should always use standard English except in foreign language classes. In this way students "hear" correct English. They should NOT be reprimanded using vulgar idioms by teachers who say that this is "all the students understand".

18. Schools should supply room furnishings, and supplies needed for each class.

This list could go on and on...add your own changes, and perhaps they will come into being someday. Changes coming are the reasons for the writing of this book. Instead of standing still, someday the school system around the world might be pushing the "PUSH" door.

Stop The Carnival!

g.d.a.

ABOUT THE AUTHOR

G. Dayhoff Addley has been writing books since the age of 16 and has had several articles with pictures published. While teaching in the Virgin Islands, she realized she would have to write down the daily humorous happenings on 3" x 5" cards in order to survive. When Ms. Addley retired, she sorted the cards chronologically and wrote them out. Too many situations escaped those cards, but any reader can see the overall picture, and those who are still there agree that *"That's the way it was and still is."* Teachers, parents and high school students everywhere will respond with feeling that *"That's the way it is everywhere!"*

Any number of books can be purchased via 1st Books, Amazon.com or BarnesAndNoble.com and other bookstores throughout the United States.

Comments will reach the author if sent via E-MAIL to dayhoffaddley@YAHOO.COM.

www.ingramcontent.com/pod-product-compliance
Lightning Source LLC
Chambersburg PA
CBHW030307290526
45785CB00001B/241

* 9 7 8 0 7 5 9 6 2 6 0 6 5 *